AF434029

PURPOSEFUL PAIN
What Your Troubles Achieve

Bryn E. MacPhail

Publisher's Cataloguing-in-Publication data
MacPhail, Bryn E.
Purposeful pain: What your troubles achieve / Bryn E. MacPhail.
Description: Nassau, BS: Media Enterprises, 2022.
p. cm.
978-976-8310-06-4

1. Consolation—Religious aspects--Christianity. 2. Suffering—
Religion. 3. Suffering—Christianity.
BV4905.B34 M334 2022
248.8/6—dc 23

Design and printing by Media Enterprises Ltd,
Cover design Beth Collins
31 Shirley Park Avenue • PO Box N-9240 • Nassau, Bahamas
Tel: 242 325 8210 • Fax: 242 325 8065
info@bahamasmedia.com • www.bahamasmedia.com

- Dedication -

To my dear wife, Allie,
Your Christ-likeness inspires me every day.
Thank you for taking this journey with me.
Proverbs 31:29

~

To my precious daughter, Anya,
You bring incalculable joy to our family.
May you always believe in Christ's daylight at midnight.
Exodus 14:14

~

In memory of Jamie Groves,
Thank you for showing me what blessing others
amid suffering looks like.
2Corinthians 4:7-12

In memory of Michael F. L. Allen,
Thank you for always reminding me where my true home lies.
Philippians 3:20-21

~

It is a joy to serve at the pleasure of the Good Shepherd.
I have been greatly blessed by the congregations that called me
to shepherd them.

St. Andrew's Presbyterian Kirk, Nassau, Bahamas
St. Giles Kingsway Presbyterian Church, Toronto, Ontario
Fraser Presbyterian Church, Tottenham, Ontario
St. Andrew's Presbyterian Church, Beeton, Ontario

- Acknowledgements -

The production of this book would not have been possible without the kind and generous support of many dear friends.

Earla Bethel
Philip Dunkley
Allen & Mary Shindler
Dr. Fendt & Deborah Shearer
Chris & Karen Carey
Duncan & Sandee Macgregor
Peter Bates & Katerina Tsavousis Bates
Dr. Magnus & Rebeca Ekedede
Marsha Stewart
Stephen & Betty Roberts
Jim & Fiona Allan
Barry & Dianne Ogle
Gavin & Carrie Collins

~

Front cover design by Beth Collins

I quickly discovered that good (and willing) proofreaders are difficult to find. I owe a huge debt of gratitude to Rev. Dr. Brian Ross for helping me with this vital component.

PURPOSEFUL PAIN
What Your Troubles Achieve

Preached on the Sundays immediately following Hurricane Dorian.

Each chapter of this book began as a sermon, preached at St. Andrew's Presbyterian Kirk in Nassau, Bahamas, between 2010 and 2020. These sermons have been adapted into a format more suitable for a book.

- Introduction -

Lord, I am willing to receive what you give;
to lack what you withhold; to relinquish what you take;
to suffer what you inflict; to be what you require.
- Jerry Bridges

I am familiar with pain and suffering. I don't want to suggest that I've suffered more than most because I'm pretty sure that's not true. And yet, I can safely say that pain has been one of the most powerful influencers in my life. God used the pain of my father's death to draw me to Himself as a young teenager. God used the pain of my fractured family to draw me into the ministry in my early twenties. And, as a Christian pastor, I've had a front row seat for observing pain in the lives of those I've sought to shepherd. Like you, I instinctively resist anything that could cause me pain or discomfort. And yet, I cannot deny that pain has profoundly shaped my character for the better. I resonate with what Pastor Alistair Begg writes, "We should neither court suffering nor complain about it. Instead, we should see it as one of the means God chooses to employ in order to make us increasingly useful to the Master" (Begg, *Made For His Pleasure*, 109).

What is striking to me is that for much of my life I was mostly oblivious to how God was using pain to make me more useful for His kingdom. I was largely unaware of how pain affected the way I did pastoral care, the way I preached, and even the way I engaged my family. I had always viewed pain as something that would produce a callous—as something that would make me stronger as I endured each season of affliction. What I discovered, however, was that pain functions more like a weight, and so there is cumulative burden to it. There came a point in 2019 when I realized I could no longer bear this weight. It had become far too heavy and it was impairing my capacity to be a useful pastor as well as be an attentive husband and father. I am grateful that God used a skilled colleague and my patient wife to help me deal with the weight of my pain. They helped me to see pain, not as something to be eliminated, but as something to be managed and leveraged for the glory of God.

It has been explained to me that in the sport of Judo you engage in combat by using your opponent's weight and strength against him while preserving your own mental and physical energy. While pain is not a personal enemy we aim to pin to the mat, I am learning to use the weight and momentum of pain in a manner that helps me to better thrive as a husband, father and pastor. In many ways, this book is my attempt to pass on some of the skills for leveraging pain that I've learned along the way. And my aim is to demonstrate how pain is a gracious gift and a primary tool that God uses to make us more like His Son, Jesus Christ.

- Chapter 1 -
When "Good People" Suffer
Job 1:1-12

The glory of God is more important than your or my comfort.
- Christopher Ash

Why should we consider the subject of pain and suffering? Why is it important? My first answer for why we should study the subject of suffering is because the Bible gives a great deal of attention to the subject. One could even say that suffering is a primary theme in Scripture. We can say this because, while the Bible is fundamentally about Christ, we cannot talk about Christ without making significant reference to His suffering.

A second reason for why we should study the subject of suffering is because *suffering is so prevalent within the human experience*. Life is hard and bad things have happened to us. Even more sobering is the fact that suffering will be a part of every person's future. Whether we have suffered much or just a little, there remains for each of us future suffering. That's not fun to hear but, intuitively, we all know this to be true.

To help us cope, many of us have learned how to set aside any thoughts about the suffering that lies ahead. I want to encourage you to take a different path. This leads me to the third reason why we should attempt to tackle this subject of suffering: I think one of the great gifts the Christian Church can give to our world is an example of how to think about, and how to live through, suffering. And, in order to provide such a testimony, it will be necessary for you to possess a perspective on suffering that is tethered to Scripture. You will need to be well-acquainted with what the Bible says about suffering. We could glean biblical principles on suffering from almost any of the sixty-six books of the Bible, but for the first few chapters of this book I'd like us to glean these principles primarily from Job.

> ~
>
> *One of the great gifts the Christian Church*
> *can give to our world is an example of how to*
> *think about, and how to live through, suffering.*
>
> ~

I don't think it is a small detail to note that Job is forty-two chapters long. That's lengthy by biblical standards. And not only is Job a long book, but it is also a slow-moving Book. After a very intense opening chapter, the Book of Job settles into a very slow pace. Why is that? Biblical commentator, Christopher Ash, gives this answer:

"Because there is no instant working through grief, no quick fix to pain, (there can be) no message of Job in a nutshell. God has given us a forty-two-chapter journey with no satisfactory bypass" (Ash, *Job*, 22).

Christopher Ash also says of the Book of Job:

"It knows what people say behind closed doors and in whispers, and it knows what we say in our tears. It is not merely an academic book. If we listen to it carefully, it will touch us, trouble us, and unsettle us at a deep level" (Ash, *Job*, 19).

While studying the Book of Job will give us a close-up encounter with the subject of suffering, I expect it should also help us to have a close-up encounter with God—and this is one of the primary aims of this book. In this chapter we'll survey the first twelve verses of the Book of Job. The Book begins:

"There was a man in the land of Uz whose name was Job, and that man was blameless and upright, one who feared God and turned away from evil" (Job 1:1).

Job: Blameless And Upright

We don't know much about Job's place of origin, but what would have been notable to the original readers is that Uz lies outside of Israel. Commentators place Job as a contemporary of Abraham, Isaac, or Jacob—not knowing precisely where to place him because we have no genealogy for Job. There is nothing in our text to suggest that Job was a Hebrew or that he had a detailed understanding of how to engage God. And yet, Job was certain that there was a God and he revered God to the degree that it affected his everyday behaviour. In short, without the advantage of coming from a privileged family or ethnicity, we would say (by our standards) that Job was "a good man".

Perhaps you are familiar with the phrase, "the great and the good". At important events, you sometimes hear it reported, "The great and the good were there." The phrase makes a distinction between people of great influence and people who are respected for their morality. The idea is that the most powerful people aren't always good people, and that good people are not always the most influential. In Job, however, we get the distinct sense that he is both. Not only is Job "blameless" and "upright" and god-fearing, but he is massively wealthy and influential too. In verse 2 and 3 we read:

"There were born to him seven sons and three daughters. He possessed 7,000 sheep, 3,000 camels, 500 yoke of oxen, and 500 female donkeys, and very many servants, so that this man was the greatest of all the people of the east."

Job is described as being "the greatest" man in the region, while also being described as a good and godly man. Job is serious about his relationship with God. In response to the regular "feasts" (i.e. parties) that his sons would host, Job is said to have consecrated his children and offered "burnt offerings" on their behalf saying, "It may be that my children have sinned, and cursed God in their hearts." The text specifies that Job did this "continually" (Job 1:5).

The first five verses of Job set the scene for us. It is a picture of "a pious man being a prosperous man" (Ash, *Job*, 35). It is a picture of how we imagine the world should be. The prosperity and ease that Job enjoys, however, is about to be profoundly interrupted. The Book of Job provides us with a unique vantage point where we find Satan and God engaged in a conversation about Job.

God's View Of Job

It is heartening to read what God thinks of Job:

"Have you considered my servant Job, that there is none like him on the earth, a blameless and upright man, who fears God and turns away from evil?" (Job 1:8)

Most people that I know care deeply about what others think of them. I certainly care about what others think of me. But what concerns me the most is what God thinks of me. Here we have an explicit description of what God thinks about Job. God is so impressed with Job and his ways that he actually boasts to Satan about him!

Satan's View Of Job

Satan is not nearly as impressed with Job. Satan believes that Job's prosperity is the only reason for his piety, and so he counters:

"Does Job fear God for no reason? Have you not put a hedge around him and his house and all that he has, on every side? You have blessed the work of his hands, and his possessions have increased in the land. But stretch out your hand and touch all that he has, and he will curse You to Your face" (Job 1:9-11).

If we aren't familiar with this story we might imagine that, in a way consistent with His character, God would tell Satan to "Get lost!" and to "Leave Job alone!" But that's not what happens. Instead, God does something that shocks most of us and shatters our expectations of how we think life should go. God says to Satan, "Behold, all that (Job) has is in your hand. Only against him do not stretch out your hand" (Job 1:12).

Challenging Common Paradigms

Many of us hold to a paradigm that says, "If we obey God and always try to do what is right then only good things will happen to us." It is easy to identify a person who subscribes to this paradigm because this is the person who is most shocked and surprised when suffering befalls them. Many harbour the conviction that good things happen to good people and bad things happen to bad people. The rise in popularity of Eastern religions in Western culture has contributed to the growing influence of this perspective. Some imagine that the Universe has a mechanism, called "karma", which metes our rewards and punishment according to what each person deserves. The Bible puts forward a very different picture—and it shocks us. *In the Bible, we see the good suffer. More than that, we see the good suffer even while they are doing what is good and right.*

What we also find is that God's purposes are always in play in human suffering. Suffering is not random, nor is it the result of mathematical probability. The Bible teaches that God's glory and honour can, and will, be advanced in the midst of human suffering. Job may be one of the earliest examples of this, but he certainly is not the only example. The story of Job prepares us for the story of Jesus. In Job, the greatest man in the land suffers great loss. In Jesus, the greatest man to ever live— the Son of God—suffers and dies on a cross.

Over the next few chapters we will continue to examine this very complex intersection—*where God's purposes meet human pain.* In doing so, we are preparing ourselves for our own day of trouble so that we too can give God the glory in it.

Chapter 2

Trusting God When He Can't Be Traced
Job 1:13-22

God is too good to be unkind and He is too wise to be mistaken.
And when we cannot trace His hand, we must trust His heart.
- Charles Spurgeon

The Book of Job shatters our paradigm of how we think life should be. Many of us harbour the conviction that if we are good people—if we try our best, if our intentions are kind—then God will bless and protect us. The story of Job turns that perspective on its head. Job is described as blameless, as upright, and as one who fears God (Job 1:1). Job is said to be "the greatest of all the people in the east" (Job 1:3). He is described as a man who is committed to worshipping God and "doing the right thing". And yet, Job suffers terribly.

An Unusual Negotiation

Job 1:6-12 provides a glimpse into an unusual exchange between God and Satan. It's not simply that it is unusual for God and Satan to have a conversation that is detailed for us in the Bible, but the nature of the conversation is also unusual. John Piper offers an illustration where he has us imagine that we are the owner of a jewelry store. We return to our store in the evening only to discover that there is a thief inside. Seeing that a thief is inside your store, would you say to him: "Hello there! What do you think of all these precious gems? Have you seen the big, beautiful, diamond in the display case to your left?"

We read about God conversing with Satan, and we instinctively want God to dropkick Satan out of His presence. Instead, God says to the thief, "Have you considered my servant Job?" (Job 1:8). God delights in Job and He praises him in the presence of Satan. Satan is not nearly as impressed with Job. Satan claims that Job's piety is merely a function of his prosperity. Satan asserts that if Job's possessions were taken away, he would curse God. Instead of disregarding Satan's challenge, God does something that shocks us. God gives Satan access to Job's family and possessions. What follows is terrifying. In four separate incidents, just about everything that Job values is taken from him.

Incalculable Loss

First, the Sabeans steal Job's oxen and donkeys and kill the servants tending to them (Job 1:15). And then Job is told of an incident where "the fire of God fell from heaven" (presumably lightning), killing his sheep and servants (Job 1:16). It is also reported that the Chaldeans steal Job's camels and kill the servants tending to them (Job 1:17). And finally, a most devastating report is delivered to Job:

"Your sons and daughters were eating and drinking wine in their oldest brother's house, and behold, a great wind came across the wilderness and struck the four corners of the house, and it fell upon the young people, and they are dead" (Job 1:18,19).

The loss of property alone is significant. When we hear of people losing everything they own from Hurricane Dorian*, our hearts sink and our sympathies are stirred. But Job did not simply lose his material possessions. Just about everyone under his employ was tragically killed. And every one of Job's ten children is killed in a single incident. How does Job respond?

Job's Response

The first part of Job's response is what we might expect—he tears his robe and shaves his head—which we assume to be a conventional way of mourning in Job's day (Job 1:20). Job is not in denial about what has just happened. He doesn't pretend that everything is just fine when it obviously isn't. But notice that there is more to Job's response than simply mourning.

"Then Job arose and tore his robe and shaved his head and fell to the ground and worshipped. And he said, 'Naked I came from my mother's womb, and naked shall I return. The Lord gave, and the Lord has taken away; blessed be the name of the Lord.'" (Job 1:20)

There are so many other ways in which Job could have responded to these tragedies. And as the Book of Job progresses we see changes in how Job responds. But Job's initial response—his instinctive response—is a profound mixture of grief and worship.

Do you see how Job's theology helps him cope with this first wave of grief? Job understands that he entered this world with nothing, and that he will leave with nothing. He understands that everything he possesses is a gift from God. And God, being God, has the right to take away.

Job eventually struggles to maintain this perspective and posture before God. We see Job begin to ask the questions and raise the objections that are likely on our minds as we consider his story. But initially, the first challenge from Satan is answered. Satan asserted that a suffering Job would curse God. Instead, we find a suffering Job giving thanks to God:

"The Lord giveth, and the Lord hath taketh away, blessed be the name of the Lord" (Job 1:21 KJV).

The next verse says, "In all this Job did not sin or charge God with wrong" (Job 1:22). Again, Job's posture will eventually falter as the pain of his loss continues to set in. But we would be remiss if we didn't take notice of Job's remarkable, initial, response to receiving the awful news of the death of his children. Job doesn't offer any explanation beyond confessing God's right as God to do as He sees fit. He doesn't articulate an understanding of why this has happened, but he does demonstrate an ongoing reliance and trust in God. In other words, Job continues to trust God even when he cannot trace His purposes.

Our Response To Suffering

What about you? Will you trust God when you cannot trace Him? Will you rely upon God even when you cannot make sense of your painful circumstances? For Job, it was his understanding of the prerogative of God that helped him to cope with his loss. For Charles Spurgeon, it was the character of God that compelled his trust: "God is too good to be unkind and He is too wise to be mistaken." That's the kind of perspective that will help us immensely in the day of trial. And the reason we are certain that God is good, and that His intentions toward us are kind, is because the Scriptures clearly reveals this. The reason we can be sure that God's wisdom never falters, or errs, is because this is what Scripture teaches.

Now, I don't want to suggest that biblical knowledge and good theology will make you impervious to the pain that accompanies suffering. But what I am saying is that we will need biblical knowledge and good theology if we are to trust God when we cannot trace Him.

We will need to be able to recall Scripture like Joshua 1:5, "Just as I was with Moses, so I will be with you. I will not leave or forsake you." We will need Psalm 34:18: "The Lord is near to the brokenhearted and saves the crushed in spirit." And Romans 8:28 (NIV): "And we know that in all things God works for the good of those who love him, who have been called according to his purpose." And 1Peter 5:7: "(Cast) all your anxieties on Him, because He cares for you."

> ~
> *We will need biblical knowledge*
> *and good theology if we are to*
> *trust God when we cannot trace Him.*
> ~

The Bible assures us of God's abiding presence, His concern for our predicament, and His control over our circumstances. What we don't get, however, is a detailed explanation of things. What we don't get from the Bible is a clear sense of why we suffer in the particular ways we do. We suffer, in general, because we live in a Fallen world that has been affected by sin. But why particular people suffer particular hardships is not detailed for us. We may not know why, but we are told what for. God's great concern, as revealed in Scripture, is His glory.

I think we should return to our original question: Will you trust God when you cannot trace Him? The Bible assures us that our sovereign God has kind intentions and righteous purposes when He allows us to suffer. The Bible also assures us that suffering will not get the final word. And remember, we have a perspective that Job lacked. *We live after the cross of Christ.* We have seen sin and evil defeated at the cross. And we've seen God's glory advanced through the suffering of His Son. We've witnessed how God can manage the worst of circumstances toward a blessed outcome.

God can be trusted with your painful circumstances. Even when we cannot trace God's particular purposes, we have every reason to trust in His character.

- **Chapter 3 -**
When Your Suffering Is Great
Job 2:1-13

*What God takes from me is less than I owe Him,
and what He leaves me is more than I deserve.
- William Gurnall*

Satan challenged God, claiming that Job's piety was simply a function of his prosperity. Satan asserted that a suffering Job would curse God. Instead, we see a suffering Job give thanks to God. Job says, "The Lord giveth, and the Lord hath taketh away, blessed be the name of the Lord" (Job 1:21 KJV).

Satan's Persistence

As we wade into Job 2, we see Satan once again present himself before God. The conversation resumes with God asking the same question that was posed in chapter one: "Have you considered my servant Job, that there is none like him on earth, a blameless and upright man, who fears God and turns away from evil?"

But now, God adds to Job's resume: "(Job) holds fast his integrity, although you incited Me against him to destroy him without reason" (Job 2:3).

Satan, still not backing down, answers the Lord: "Skin for skin! All that a man has he will give for his life. But stretch out your hand and touch his bone and his flesh, and he will curse you to your face" (Job 2:4,5).

Satan makes a distinction between what a person *has*, and what a person *is*. While it is certainly painful to lose what we have, the assertion being made is that Job's faith in God would not survive a direct attack against himself.

Suffering Carefully Measured

We are faced with a similarly somber scenario as we had in the previous chapter. Satan wants to harm Job. Shockingly, God gives Satan a measure of access to do so. If we don't know how the story goes, we might expect God to say something like: "That's enough Satan. You were wrong about Job. He proved you wrong. Now, get out of here!" Instead, we read: "the Lord said to Satan, "Behold, he is in your hand; only spare his life""(Job 2:6).

There is something that is both terrifying and comforting in what God does here. What is terrifying is that God gives Satan permission to harm Job. And yet, what is comforting is to know that *Satan requires permission from God* in order to harm Job. It is comforting to know that God, in His sovereign wisdom, has placed limits upon what the enemy can do.

With the limits set, we are told, "Satan went out from the presence of the Lord and struck Job with loathsome sores from the sole of his foot to the crown of his head. And (Job) took a piece of broken pottery with which to scrape himself while he sat in the ashes" (Job 2:7,8).

In Mourning

What a miserable scene! Job has already torn his clothes and shaved his head as part of his mourning process. Now he is pictured sitting on the ground, in a pile of ashes, covered in sores, treating himself with a broken piece of pottery.

To our modern ears this may seem a bit excessive. We need to keep bringing to our minds what Job has lost. All of Job's possessions have been taken or destroyed. Job's servants and all ten of his children have been killed. Job is languishing and his physical appearance is mirroring his inward grief.

Job's wife makes her approach and says, "Do you still hold fast your integrity? Curse God and die" (Job 2:9). In spite of their enormous loss, Job still challenges his wife—Job claims that she is speaking as a "foolish" person for urging him to curse God. Job goes on to ask (and I think the NIV reads better on this): "Shall we accept good from God, and not trouble?" (Job 2:10).

What a remarkable perspective! Here in The Bahamas it is common to hear a person exclaim, "God is good". Of course, this is a wonderful statement to make. But when do we typically hear that statement uttered? Isn't it almost always when some-thing good happens to us? Job has something to teach us here. God's goodness should not be tethered to our personal circum-stances. In the best of times and in the worst of times, "God is good". As the song goes, "God is good all the time". Or, as Job puts it: "The Lord giveth, and the Lord has taken away; blessed be the name of the Lord."

The scene then shifts with the arrival of Job's three friends: Eliphaz, Bildad, and Zophar (Job 2:11). As the story unfolds we will see that these three friends challenge Job in in-appropriate ways and ultimately prove to be unhelpful comfort-ers. But they begin well. We are told, "They made an appoint-ment together to come to show sympathy and comfort him" (Job 2:11). Job's friends begin with honourable intentions:

"And when they saw (Job) from a distance, they did not recognize him. And they raised their voices and wept, and they tore their robes and sprinkled dust on their heads toward heaven. And they sat with him on the ground seven days and seven nights, and no one spoke a word to him, for they saw that his suffering was very great" (Job 2:12,13).

Job's friends begin with what appears to be sincere acts of empathy. They sit on the ground with him. "No one spoke a word to (Job), for they saw that his suffering was very great." This is an example that I wish more Christians would be careful to replicate. When our loved ones are suffering, do not come armed with clichés and explanations. And, at least initially, resist the temptation to share every relevant Bible verse that comes to your mind. When your friend's suffering is great, it is enough to show up and to sit quietly and to pray silently.

Satan's Strategy

I want to circle back to how the suffering all began for Job. If you are like me, the idea of Satan challenging God and asking for access to Job is quite unsettling. It's perhaps even more startling to observe how God grants Satan access to Job, albeit with some limitations. Christopher Ash, notes the same when he writes:

"The book of Job is a scary book…because of the real understanding that this terrible story may in some way become our story too. Our horror in reading the story of Job is more than an empathetic horror; it is a personal horror" (Ash, *Job*, 55).

We want to believe that the story of Job is exceptional and not indicative of what we will experience. You will be pleased to hear that, in many ways, the story of Job is exceptional and is not intended to be normative for the follower of Jesus. The fall of Job, and the particular losses he endured, are not what you should expect to experience.

The story of a righteous Job who suffers so terribly is intended to prepare us for the story of Jesus. And yet, what appears to be normative is this notion that God allows the enemy to send trials our way. This is evidenced most clearly in the New Testament, when Jesus says to Peter and the disciples: "Satan demanded to have you, that he might sift you like wheat" (Lk. 22:31). The word "you" in the original Greek is in the plural form. Satan not only wants to sift Peter, but all who would line up as followers of Jesus. And notice how Jesus finishes His statement to Peter. Jesus doesn't say, "Peter, Satan demanded to have you, that he might sift you like wheat, but don't worry, My Father won't let this happen." I think many of us would like to see a verse that says that Satan no longer has the access and ability to send trials our way. Unfortunately, no such assurances are given. We are assured, however, that when we are being tested, we have an Advocate. "(Peter), Satan demanded to have you, that he might sift you like wheat, but I have prayed for you that your faith may not fail."

Our enemy sends trials in an attempt to destroy our faith. God's intentions, as you would expect, are markedly different. God's purpose in allowing the enemy to set trials before us is to strengthen our faith and dependence upon Him. And, how we fare in the trials pivots, in a huge way, on the advocacy of Jesus.

*God's purpose in allowing the enemy to set trials before us
is to strengthen our faith and dependence upon Him.*

Jesus' Advocacy

Are you in trouble? Are you hurting? Are you experiencing trials and temptations? May it hearten you to hear: *Jesus is praying for you.* Jesus is praying that your faith will not fail. Robert McCheyne once said: "If I could hear Christ praying for me in the next room, I would not fear a million of enemies… (And) He is praying for me."

It may be the case that your suffering has been great. Or, great suffering may be a present reality for you. Either way, it is important for you to have this confidence: You are not alone. You have a Divine Advocate for whom the enemy is no match. Your being sifted is but for a season. You have good reason to believe that your faith will not fail. Jesus is praying. Jesus is praying *for you.*

- Chapter 4 -
Uncensored Grief
Job 3

My dear friend, when grief presses you to the dust,
worship there!
- Charles Spurgeon

In the first two chapters of Job we watched an upright and God-fearing man suffer terribly. Job, whom God considered blameless, has his possessions taken away, his ten children killed, and his health compromised. Satan challenged God, asserting that a suffering Job would curse God. Job, however, maintains his integrity and his trust in God. Upon hearing the horrible news of all that he had lost, Job declares:

"Naked I came from my mother's womb, and naked shall I return. The Lord gave, and the Lord has taken away; blessed be the name of the Lord" (Job 1:21).

And when his own health fails, and his wife urges him to curse God, Job responds:

"Shall we accept good from God, and not trouble?" (Job 2:10).

Job's response to what he has lost is remarkable. But, as we might expect, Job's grief intensifies. In chapter 2, Job is depicted in torn clothes, with a shaved head, sitting on the ground—in a pile of ashes—scratching at his sores with a piece of broken pottery. It's a miserable scene. Three of Job's friends arrive on the scene and sit with him. And not a word is spoken for "seven days and seven nights" (Job 2:13).

We come to chapter 3 and, finally, Job is ready to speak. Job is no longer able to contain his anguish. Christopher Ash describes Job 3 as "the darkest chapter of the Book". Job doesn't hold back. His words are not sanitized—they are not filtered. Job has lost far too much to say less than how he really feels. While there is much to be gleaned from Job 3, I'd like to highlight four principles:

1) It is a normal thing for a Christian to express unhappiness and grief
2) It is a normal thing for a Christian to be unsettled by suffering
3) Why our perseverance in suffering is important
4) How to persevere through terrible suffering

Grief Expressed

First—*it is a normal thing for a believer to express unhappiness and grief.* This is important to note in the face of certain cultures within the church that do not allow for (or encourage) such expressions. Presbyterians, for example, with our Scottish heritage, have in many contexts mastered the art of suppressing grief. With our strong theology and our understanding of God's sovereignty, we have trained ourselves to bravely accept whatever is thrown our way. Many Presbyterians resonate with Job's opening words: "The Lord gave, and the Lord has taken away;

blessed be the name of the Lord" (Job 1:21). But many of these same Presbyterians wouldn't dream of expressing their grief in the uncensored manner we see from Job in chapter 3:

"Let the day perish on which I was born, and the night that said, 'A man is conceived.' Let that day be darkness! May God above not seek it, nor light shine upon it. Let gloom and deep darkness claim it. Let the clouds dwell upon it; let the blackness of the day terrify it" (Job 3:3-5).

Here we see that Job finally begins to curse. Job does not curse God—as Satan predicted he would—but Job does curse "the day of his birth" (Job 3:1). Job doesn't challenge God directly, but he does appear to be challenging God's governance of things. This is our first glimpse of Job struggling to maintain his composure. We marvel at Job's initial composure, and yet it is not right for us to insist that he remain composed. Job does not bottle up his grief indefinitely, and neither should we. King David, in Psalm 39, describes the futility of keeping everything inside when he writes:

"I was mute and silent; I held my peace to no avail, and my distress grew worse. My heart became hot within me. As I mused, the fire burned; then I spoke with my tongue" (Ps. 39:2-3).

There remains a culture within some churches where the expectation is that everything be kept inside. In other traditions, where a theology of "health, wealth, and prosperity" carries the day, grief and lament are similarly denied entry. This is not something that Scripture commends. Nor is this the example that Jesus provides. At His approach to the tomb of Lazarus, we are told, "Jesus wept" (John 11:35). We need to let our thoughts linger with that statement. The second member of the Trinity, the Creator of the Universe, the Saviour of the world—is *weeping* at the grave of a friend. Keep in mind that this is the One who has authority over life and death. Jesus knows full well that in a few minutes Lazarus will be alive again, and yet at the sight of His friend's tomb, in the midst of a gathering of mourners, Jesus weeps. Indeed, *it is a normal thing for a Christian to express unhappiness and grief.*

Not At Ease

Similarly, *it is a normal thing for a Christian to be un-settled by suffering.* The distinction I make between these two points is a distinction between *expression* and *disposition.* The first point relates primarily to what we *say*, or *do*, as a result of our grief. The second point relates to how our suffering makes us *feel.* Again, we are not to take the posture of an unfeeling sto-ic. Death and loss hurt, and we are supposed to feel unsettled by these things. Listen to Job's own words at the end of the chapter:

"For my sighing comes instead of my bread, and my groan-ings are poured out like water. For the thing that I fear comes upon me, and what I dread befalls me. I am not at ease, nor am I quiet; I have no rest, but trouble comes" (Job 3:24-26).

These are not easy things for a person to admit. Imagine you greet me, "Good morning, Pastor, how are you today?" And I respond by saying to you, "Awful—just awful. My groanings are poured out like water. The thing I fear has come upon me, and I am not at ease." Many of us are not equipped for that kind of conversation. We've been told to "put our best face on", to always smile, and to tell everyone that we are doing just fine. The reality is, however, that life is hard and we are not always fine. And that's okay. That's normal. Job was a righteous, God-fearing, man, and yet he knew what it was like not to be at ease. Even the great apostle Paul knew what is was like to be unsettled by suffering. Paul tells the Corinthians: "For when we came into Macedonia, we had no rest, but we were harassed at every turn—conflicts on the outside, fears within" (2Cor. 7:5 NIV). *It is a normal thing for a Christian to be unsettled by suffering.*

Honoring God Amid Suffering

As I say that, however, I wouldn't want you to think that any and every response to suffering is equally appropriate. This leads me to our third principle: *Why our perseverance in suffering is important.* The most succinct answer I can give is to say that *how you respond to suffering can profoundly help or hinder your testimony as a Christian.* To use John Piper's words, "If you are bitter at God you're not going to lead anyone to Jesus."

~
How you respond to suffering can profoundly help or hinder your testimony as a Christian.
~

Seasons of suffering provide opportunities for believers to demonstrate just how much we treasure Jesus. And if you don't treasure Jesus more than you treasure your health or your wealth, you will struggle to effectively commend Jesus to others. But let me frame this with a positive example. When I was in my early twenties, I had a very good friend who was dying of cancer. I was a few years older than Jamie Groves, but having been his instructor at Muskoka Woods (summer camp), and then moving to the same town as he, Jamie and I had many opportunities to spend time together. Now, when you are eighteen years old and dying of cancer, you could be excused if you were angry, or bitter, or if you just wanted to be left alone. But not Jamie Groves. Jamie wanted people around. In particular, Jamie was concerned about friends and family members who did not yet have a relationship with Jesus. To this end, Jamie determined to purchase and distribute several copies of C.S. Lewis' book, "Mere Christianity" so that others might be encouraged to trust and treasure Jesus as he did. The effect of Jamie's testimony, and this gesture, was significant. And even today, many years after his death, the account of Jamie Groves' Christian testimony and his response to suffering continues to be a story that is repeated among the staff at Muskoka Woods in Rosseau, Ontario.

It is important that, ultimately, we view our season of suffering as an opportunity to glorify God by continuing to treasure Jesus Christ above all else. And since we might not begin with that perspective, it is important that we talk about *how to persevere through terrible suffering*. You might be pleased to hear that I'm not going to recommend a 12-step plan for you to follow. As I review the Scriptures, I see *two things* in particular that are vital to our perseverance amid suffering. I'd like to return to Psalm 39 once again—this time looking at verse 7, where David confesses, "And now, O Lord, for what do I wait? My hope is in you." The place where we need to begin is to *see God as your one true hope*.

Our Only Hope For Enduring

Over the course of our life, we learn to place our trust in many things and in many people. We depend upon certain friends to help us when we are in trouble, we depend upon our spouse, we depend upon our parents for help when we are younger, and we often depend upon our children for assistance when we are older. We turn to doctors when we are not well, and we trust that their prescription of medical treatment will be of some benefit to us. These things are all good and fine, but none of these things is big enough to serve as our ultimate hope. *In order to persevere in the day of trial you will need God to be your ultimate hope.* In order for you to maintain a compelling testimony amid suffering, you will need to be able to say with David, "My hope is in you." This is the first thing we must do.

The second thing we must do is *we must cry out to God for help.* Look at Psalm 39:12: "Hear my prayer, O Lord, and give ear to my cry; hold not your peace at my tears!" If you close your Bible at the end of Psalm 39 you are left wondering how things ended for David. Did God hear David's cry? Don't close your Bible at the end of Psalm 39! Look at the first few verses of Psalm 40:

> *"I waited patiently for the Lord; He inclined to me and heard my cry. He drew me up from the pit of destruction, out of the miry bog, and set my feet upon a rock, making my steps secure. He put a new song in my mouth, a song of praise to our God. Many will see and fear, and put their trust in the Lord"* (Ps. 40:1-3).

As we are finding out in our study of Job, *the road of suffering can be a long road.* What I want you to see is that you are not alone in this journey. I want you to see that there is a Helper at hand. Make Jesus Christ your one true hope. Cry out to Him in your day of trouble. If you do this, you can expect to see a day when He will *set your feet upon a rock* and a day when *He will put a new song in your mouth*. Others will see this and they will *put their trust in the Lord.*

- Chapter 5 -
When Friends Make Suffering Worse
Job 4-20

Bad theology will complicate and worsen your suffering.
- Paul David Tripp

Job has experienced profound loss. All of Job's possessions are either stolen or destroyed. Most of Job's servants are killed. All ten of Job's children are killed in a single incident. And then Job himself is afflicted with terrible sores from head to toe. By the end of chapter 2, the picture of Job we are presented with is a miserable one. His clothes are torn and he has shaved his head. Job is sitting on the ground, in a pile of ashes, and he is scraping his sores with a broken piece of pottery. Some friends appear, and they sit with him on the ground for a week, "and no one spoke a word to (Job), for they saw that his suffering was great" (Job 2:13).

In chapter 3 we finally hear Job speak. Job's suffering is indeed "great", and it is regrettable that his friends are completely inept in their attempts to bring some measure of comfort.

We are able to assess how Job's friends respond to his suffering as we glean from Job chapters 4 through 20. There is a cycle of speeches—Eliphaz, Bildad, and Zophar take turns providing their opinions for why Job is suffering as he is. Job, in turn, replies to each. The exchanges between Job and his friends are both awkward and ugly. The exchanges are awkward in that there is such glaring insensitivity in what Job's "friends" say and propose. And the exchanges are ugly in that they represent some of the worst ways a person could respond to a friend in pain. This section of Scripture also reminds us that we can't read every portion of Scripture is if it were overtly prescribing behaviour for us to emulate. Huge portions of Job are there to show us what *not* to believe, and what *not* to say. Christopher Ash describes what is said in these exchanges as "by and large, a load of rubbish" (Ash, *Job*, 90). And yet, not entirely so!

There are things we read in these chapters that are consistent with the wider testimony of Scripture. It would be so much easier if it were all rubbish. But isn't that our challenge with false teaching? False teaching—such as the so-called "health, wealth, and prosperity gospel"—leads many astray because it has threads of truth within it. Similarly, Job's friends aren't blatant heretics. Some of the underpinnings of their theology are sound.

When Theology Is Weaponized

Eliphaz, Bildad, and Zophar have at least two things correct as they assess Job's predicament. First, Job's *friends believe that God is absolutely in control.* Those within the Reformed tradition readily confess the same, citing the *Westminster Confession of Faith*, chapter 3, under the heading, "Of God's Eternal Decree":

God from all eternity did, by the most wise and holy counsel of His own will, freely, and unchangeably ordain whatsoever comes to pass.

Secondly, Eliphaz, Bildad, and Zophar share the Christian belief that *God is entirely just and fair*. And yet, these men struggle to believe that Job might be innocent, and undeserving, of his suffering. Listen to Eliphaz's rebuke:

"You are impatient...Is not your fear of God your confidence?...Remember: who that was innocent ever perished?... As I have seen, those who plow iniquity and sow trouble reap the same" (Job 4:5-8).

There is almost a mocking tone in this. "Job, I thought you were a godly man, why are you so upset?" And in a somewhat passive-aggressive way, Eliphaz suggests that Job's predicament is a function of what he deserves. Bildad's counsel follows a similar pattern:

"If your children have sinned against (God), He has delivered them into the hand of their transgression" (Job 8:4).

Do you see how harsh that is? Bildad is essentially saying, "Your children got what they deserved." Zophar takes a kind of passive-aggressive approach when he says:

"If iniquity is in your hand, put it far away, and not let injustice dwell in your tents" (11:14).

In other words, "Before anything else bad happens, Job you need to put away the sin in your life." This is just a small sampling of the awful things suggested by Job's friends. It's amazing that they are called "friends"! You will be glad to know that Job is no shrinking violet. Job does not pull punches in his reply to his companions:

"As for you, you whitewash with lies; worthless physicians are you all. Oh that you would keep silent, and it would be your wisdom!" (Job 13:4,5).

And in 16:2, Job similarly answers:

"I have heard many such things; miserable comforters are you all."

The "pastoral visit" by Job's friends is among the most unhelpful pastoral visits ever recorded. It's an absolute train-wreck. And yet, there are important principles for us to glean from these chapters.

Limited Perspective And Limiting Words

First, *we must not presume to know the precise reasons why a person is suffering.* As I look back on twenty-plus years of pastoral ministry, I have very few answers for why particular people suffered in the particular ways they did. Sure, in some instances, certain actions or behaviour, led individuals down a particular path—but even then, I can't pretend to know precisely why God allowed things to unfold the way they did. The Bible tells us a great deal about who God is and what He is like, and yet He is so far beyond us that we must not presume to be able to trace the specifics of His purposes. Even Paul, the most prolific New Testament writer, proclaims to the Christians in Rome:

"Oh, the depths of the riches and wisdom and knowledge of God! How unsearchable are His judgments and how inscrutable His ways! 'For who has known the mind of the Lord, or who has been His counselor?'" (Rom. 11:33,34).

Our friends in pain are not helped when we give them theories and explanations. *We must not presume to know the precise reasons why a person is suffering.* Secondly, *we must learn to talk less and sit in silence more.* Job's three friends began well. At the end of chapter 2, Job's friends weep, and mourn, and sit with Job on the ground without saying anything. Eliphaz, Bildad, and Zophar only become a problem for Job when they begin talking. As someone who enjoys talking, and as someone who talks for a living, this is something about which I have to be intentional. Over the course of my ministry, I have sat with hundreds of hurting families and individuals and not once have I regretted sitting in silence—but I have, on many occasions, wondered if I said too much or if I said something that was less than helpful. C.S. Lewis describes how the presence of others affected him after the death of his wife:

> "I find it hard to take in what anyone says. Or perhaps, hard to want to take it in. It is so uninteresting. Yet I want the others to be about me. I dread the moments when the house is empty. If only they would talk to one another and not to me" (Lewis, *A Grief Observed*, 3).

By way of background, I was ordained by the *Presbyterian Church in Canada* at the age of twenty-five. I think there will be special rewards in heaven for my first Session (Elders Board) for putting up with a precocious twenty-five-year-old pastor. Fresh off my seminary training and ordination exams, I imagined that I had a tidy theological answer for just about every question and every situation. That abruptly changed the day I got a phone call informing me that a young couple from the congregation had a baby—but the baby subsequently died just minutes after being born. I remember what it was like sitting with the grieving parents as though it were yesterday. I had no answers. I had no words. I just sat with them. It wasn't that long after conducting a funeral for this couple's baby girl, when I got a call from the local funeral home asking me to officiate at another funeral. This time it was for a twelve-year-old boy who died in a car accident. These two experiences, very early in ministry, taught me that there was a lot that I didn't know and suffering that I couldn't explain. And these two experiences convinced me of the necessity of showing up, and saying as little as possible.

There were probably other experiences, where I should I have said less, or I should have said something different than what I did. Every situation elicits a slightly different response from us. But *if we learn anything from Job's companions we learn of the unhelpfulness of persistent talking and offering theological theories and clichés when the pain of loss is still raw.*

Just because something is true doesn't mean it is timely to say. Even if you have a plausible explanation, this doesn't mean you should offer it to a friend in pain. In my third decade of marriage, Allie is still reminding me that I don't need to verbalize everything that my mind conceives, regardless of how accurate my assessment may be. This is good advice. James urges us in this direction when he writes:

Let every person be quick to hear, slow to speak, slow to anger. (Jas. 1:19).

~

*If we learn anything from Job's companions
we learn of the unhelpfulness of persistent talking
and offering theological theories and clichés
when the pain of loss is still raw.*

~

We should aim to represent the love and concern of God to our friends who are hurting. Go to them. Sit with them. Listen to them. And be slow—be very slow—to speak.

- Chapter 6 -
What Did I Do To Deserve This?
Job 31

If you ask, "Why is this happening?" no light may come, but if you ask, "How am I to glorify God now?" there will always be an answer.
- J.I. Packer

It is a normal thing to try and understand *why* suffering occurs. It is natural to want to discover the causes of our suffering in order to help us find a remedy for it. The Bible, however, does not present a neat and tidy formula to help us understand all of the reasons for suffering. By all appearances, the reasons for suffering differ greatly. In the New Testament, we have the example of a man born blind. The disciples turn to Jesus and ask:

"'Rabbi, who sinned, this man or his parents, that he was born blind?' Jesus answered, 'It was not that this man sinned, or his parents, but that the works of God might be displayed in him'" (Jn. 9:2,3).

Jesus proceeds to put mud on the man's eyes, instructs him to go wash, and the man comes back seeing (Jn. 9:7). In this instance, there is no connection between sin and suffering. But, sometimes, there is a connection. Pastor Alistair Begg often makes a distinction between "the suffering we *meet*" and "the suffering we *make*". If you follow the story of Jonah, or if you track with King David after committing adultery with Bathsheba, it's impossible to miss the connection between their disobedience and the suffering that follows. Much of the time, however, it is difficult to trace the origin of our suffering to something we have done. Much of the time the reason for our suffering is veiled. But still, we ask the question: *What did I do to deserve this?*

Job's companions—Eliphaz, Bildad, and Zophar—had asserted that Job must have done something awful and that is why his suffering was so great. There is evidence that Job had thought deeply on what his friends asserted because what we have in chapter 31 is not a knee-jerk, off-the-cuff, response to his accusers. Rather, Job lays out a very detailed, and comprehensive defense for how he has lived his life.

Job's Defense

Job opens chapter 31 with a phrase that has come into popular use for Christians in our day. Job says, "I have made a covenant with my eyes" (Job 31:1). Job's point is that he is not superficial in his fidelity toward his wife. Job makes every effort to not even *look* at another woman inappropriately. Job articulates his understanding that nothing is hidden from God when he asks rhetorically in verse 4, "Does not he see my ways and number all my steps?" Job has been so disciplined that he says that not even his "heart" has been "enticed toward (another) woman" (Job 31:9). Suffice to say, this is more than many men could claim. Job was faithful to his wife.

Job insists that he has never rejected the cause of his servants and has been diligent in listening to their concerns (Job 31:13,14). He asserts that he has been attentive to the needs of others and has not "withheld anything that the poor desired", nor has he done anything to cause "the eyes of the widow to fail" (Job 31:16). Job notes that he has provided food and clothing to the "fatherless" and to those in need (Job 31:17-22). Job indicates that his motivation for acting in this manner was his fear that God would judge him harshly if he did otherwise (Job 31:23).

Job maintains that he has not "made gold his trust", nor has he "rejoiced that (his) wealth was abundant" (Job 31:24,25). Job was very wealthy, but apparently this wasn't something he focused on—this is not how Job identified himself. In the New Testament, Jesus warns: "No one can serve two masters…You cannot serve God and money" (Matt. 6:24). This was not a problem for Job. Job's trust was in God, and not in money. He insists that he has been gracious to his enemies (Job 31:29-30) and hospitable to strangers (Job 31:31-32). He has observed how many conceal their transgressions, and how many hide their iniquity—but Job maintains that he has nothing to hide (Job 31:33).

Job is quite thorough in his self-assessment. In Job's mind, there is nothing he has done that would warrant the suffering he has endured. His defense is entirely predicated on the assumption that good things happen to good people and bad things happen to bad people and, by this standard Job demands an explanation from God.

What we learn in the Book of Job, however, is that there are not neat and tidy connections between godliness and prosperity and godlessness and suffering. Sometimes the wicked prosper. And sometimes the righteous suffer. Accordingly, when you ask "Why?" or when you ask, "What did I do to deserve this?" there is a really good possibility that you won't get a clear answer. However, I do think the example of Jesus healing the blind man in John 9 does give us a reliable template. The disciples, like Job's companions, held to a worldview that says you get what you deserve in life. Jesus refutes that worldview saying, "It was not that this man sinned, or his parents, but that the works of God might be displayed in him." This suggests that, while there may not always be a clear answer to "Why?" we suffer in the particular ways we do, there is a "What for" aspect that relates to the glory and honour of the God we worship.

When suffering comes, will your faith in the goodness of God remain steadfast? Will you worship God even when you are hurting badly? Job does remarkably well given all that he has suffered. Not only does he lose all of his possessions, but also most of his servants are killed, along with his seven sons and three daughters. On top of all that, Job then has to deal with terrible sores and terrible friends.

Is It Acceptable To Rail Against God?

While Job maintains a steady faith in God for the most part, we see Job's trust in God come off the rails near the end of this chapter. Having completed his self-evaluation, Job challenges God:

"Oh, that I had one to hear me! (Here is my signature! Let the Almighty answer me!) Oh, that I had the indictment written by my adversary! Surely I would carry it on my shoulder; I would bind it on me as a crown; I would give him an account of all my steps; like a prince I would approach him" (31:35-37).

This is beyond bold. Job is calling out God. Job is using courtroom language here, and he actually believes he has a winning case against God. On a few occasions I have heard individuals say something like: "When I get to heaven, God has some explaining to do!" Or, "When I get to meet God, I need Him to answer some questions for me!" Let me assure you; the conversation is not going to go like that. I have also heard people suggest that it is quite acceptable to complain to God—pointing to the many examples in the Bible, where God's people complain to God about their circumstances. Indeed—from Job to Moses to King David to the prophet Jeremiah—there is no shortage of people who have grumbled against God and made serious complaints. However, by the time you get to Job 38, it becomes clear that Job is completely out of line in challenging God to give an account.

Again, it is important to remember that, when we read the Bible, distinctions need to be made between what is *prescriptive* and what is *descriptive*. There are times when the Bible is *prescribing* things for us to do, and there are times when the Bible is simply *describing* what has taken place. And, sometimes, the description is there to show us what *not* to do! Job's defiance and his challenge to God is *not a prescription* of what we should do when we suffer. Job's defiance and challenge to God shows us what *not* to do.

Wrestle with God in prayer. Be honest with Him about how you are feeling (He already knows how you feel!). But don't forget with Whom you are speaking. When we pray, we are praying to the One who made the Universe and all that is within it. We are praying to the One who created us, and who sustains our life, moment by moment.

Wrestle with God in prayer. Be honest with Him about how you are feeling (He already knows how you feel!). But don't forget with Whom you are speaking.

Appreciating the One with Whom we are speaking will affect our posture, our tone, and our requests. Our approach should be a mix of awe and adoration. One of my favourite scenes in *The Lion, The Witch And The Wardrobe* cleverly captures a proper approach:

Susan: "Is he—quite safe? I shall feel rather nervous about meeting a lion."

"That you will, dearie, and no mistake," said Mrs. Beaver. "If there's anyone who can appear before Aslan without their knees knocking, they're either braver than most or else just silly."

"Then he isn't safe?" said Lucy.

"Safe?" said Mr. Beaver; "don't you hear what Mrs. Beaver tells you? Who said anything about safe? 'Course he isn't safe. But he's good. He's the King, I tell you."

The life and testimony of Job dramatically confirms that God is not "safe" as we understand safe. *But He's good. He's the King, I tell you.*

- Chapter 7 -
God's Answer For Your Pain
Job 38-41

*When we suffer, we must trust that God knows what He is do-
ing, and that He works in and through the pain and afflictions
of His people for His glory and for their sanctification.*
- R.C. Sproul

Job has endured unimaginable loss. All of his children are
dead—seven sons and three daughters, killed in a single incident. Job's wealth has been confiscated, most of his servants have been killed, and even his own health has been compromised. Job has torn his clothes and shaved his head in mourning.
He is sitting on the ground in a pile of ashes, and with a broken
piece of pottery, he is scratching the sores that cover his body.
Job is soon joined by three friends, Eliphaz, Bildad, and Zophar;
but ultimately they add to Job's misery. Job, naturally, wants
answers. He wants to know what he has done to deserve such
pain and suffering. Much of the Book is a poetic cycle of con-
versations between Job and his companions. As Job continues to
ask "Why?", his companions, in turn, bring forward their theories. You could summarize the responses of Job's companions
by saying that they believe Job must have done something to
deserve this. Their worldview is not unlike what many hold to
today—that good things happen to good people, and bad things
happen to bad people. Job's friends are of the view that this is

how God operates.

Eliphaz, Bildad, and Zophar don't have a category to explain how a person of integrity could suffer to the extent that Job has. Accordingly, Job's friends continue to probe for some secret sin. Job calls them "miserable comforters" (Job 16:2) and, in chapter 31, he makes his final defense. Using courtroom language, Job challenges God to appear and to give an account for Himself (Job 31:35). This definitely falls into the category of "Be careful what you ask for".

God's Reply To Job

In chapter 38, God appears and replies to Job. God's response spans four chapters and is the longest speech by God recorded in the Old Testament. In the New Testament we talk about the "Sermon on the Mount" being the longest recorded speech by Jesus. Job 38 through 41 is the Old Testament counterpart (in terms of length). I commend these chapters to your reading—they are worship-inducing, to be sure. Here is a sample of God's reply:

38:4,5
"Where were you when I laid the foundation of the earth? Tell me, if you have understanding. Who determined its measurements—surely you know!"

38:11
"(Have you said to the sea), "Thus far shall you come, and no farther, and here shall your proud waves be stayed?"

38:12
"Have you commanded the morning since your days began,

and caused the dawn to know its place?"

38:31
"Can you bind the chains of Pleiades or loose the cords of Orion?"

In chapter 39, God names a variety of species from the animal kingdom and asks Job what influence he had on their origin and on their behaviour. God's response to Job is substantial. God being God was not obligated to say anything to Job. The fact that God replies to Job, and does so in such a detailed way, is a gracious condescension. And given the length of this reply, isn't it striking that God does not directly answer Job's question?

Job wants to know "Why?"—Job wants *an explanation* for his dreadful predicament, but none is given. *Instead of revealing to Job an answer, God reveals Himself to Job.* Instead of answering the "Why?" God answers the "Whom?" And what we learn from this is that our deepest concerns are satisfied in the experience of God's presence and not in possessing explanations for our problems. Given what God has said, Job's response is fitting:

"Then Job answered the Lord and said: 'Behold, I am of small account; what shall I answer you? I lay my hand on my mouth. I have spoken once, and I will not answer; twice, but I will proceed no further" (Job 40:4,5).

> ~
> *Our deepest concerns are satisfied*
> *in the experience of God's presence*
> *and not in possessing explanations for our problems.*
> ~

The Answer For Our Pain Is Not What We Expected

When we suffer, we naturally want answers. We naturally want an explanation for *why* we are going through what we are. And since we regard God as all-knowing and all-powerful, it is reasonable on one level that we would want to hear from Him. It is precisely because we believe that God governs carefully, and does all things well, that we come to Him looking to understand what is taking place. And yet, if the Book of Job teaches us anything—if these four chapters teach us anything—it is that we do not need the answers we are seeking. It is enough if we meet with God. R.C. Sproul frames this well when he writes:

"Ultimately the only answer God gave Job was a revelation of Himself. It was as if God said to him, "Job, *I* am your answer." Job was not asked to trust a plan but a person, a personal God who is sovereign, wise, and good" (Sproul, *Surprised By Suffering*, 34).

C.S. Lewis similarly concludes: "I know now, Lord, why you utter no answer. You are yourself the answer. Before your face questions die away. What other answer would suffice?"

~

We do not need the answers we are seeking.
It is enough if we meet with God.

~

Even amid the greatest hardship, we can be satisfied by the Lord's presence. This is our great consolation in suffering. Your suffering, your pain—the bad things that have happened in your life—are *not* God's way of punishing you for things you've done, or not done. Nor is your suffering random—your pain is not beyond God's ability to control and limit. Nineteenth Century preacher, Charles Spurgeon, puts it this way:

"It would be a very sharp and trying experience to me to think that I have an affliction which God never sent me, that the bitter cup was never filled by his hand, that my trials were never measured out by him, nor sent to me by his arrangement of their weight and quantity."

Spurgeon goes on to say:

"If our great pains were not regulated by (Divine) wisdom, we might be alarmed at them, but now we need not be afraid . . . He who made no mistakes in balancing the clouds and meting out the heavens, commits no errors in measuring out the ingredients which compose the medicine of souls."

You might be struggling immensely at the moment. It may be difficult to see the proverbial "light at the end of the tunnel" or the "silver lining" in your circumstances. But if Job teaches us anything it is that our most urgent task is to trust God in the day of trial. God is big enough and powerful enough that He can turn bad things into good things.

The Strength Of God's Arm

Of all the metaphors that God employs in His response to Job, one that lingers with me is found in 40:9. God asks Job, "Have you an *arm* like God?" From ancient times to even today, *the arm* has been a primary indicator of a person's strength. When I began weightlifting with my friends as a teenager, the way we would measure our progress was by flexing our biceps and making comparisons. Sometimes we would arm-wrestle to determine who was the strongest among us. Unfortunately, with each passing year I note that my arm strength is diminishing. These days my arms get tired bringing the groceries in from the car. My arms have limited strength. Similarly, I have a very limited capacity to govern the circumstances of my life. There is so much that is beyond my control. There is so much in life that I cannot lift. But then along comes God, who asks, "Do you have an arm like Me?"

I realize that this is anthropomorphic language and that God doesn't actually have arms like us. But God uses these human images to convey to us what He is capable of. Throughout the Old Testament, the most common use of the metaphor of an "arm" is to describe how God redeems and delivers His people. In Psalm 44, the Psalmist confesses:

"It was not by their sword that they won the land, nor did their arm bring them victory; it was your right hand, (it was) your arm" (Ps. 44:3, NIV).

And in Isaiah 51, where future assistance is promised, the LORD declares:

"My righteousness draws near speedily, my salvation is on the way, and my arm will bring justice to the nations. The islands will look to me and wait in hope for my arm" (Isa. 51:5, NIV).

If God's arm is not strong, then we can have no assurance that everything will work out fine in the end. Thankfully, the Bible is replete with accounts testifying to the strength of God's arm. And what we need to be reminded of is this: *God's arm is strong for you*. You may be struggling. You may be languishing in some challenging circumstances at the moment. You may be coming to grips with your inability to change your circumstances. Remember God's reply to Job: "Have you an arm like God?"

God's arm is working for you. You don't need answers and explanations as much as you need God. He is the answer. Hope in Him.

- Chapter 8 -
Suffering In The Light Of The Cross
Job 42:10-17

*Jesus came because there is something broken inside us
that can only be, will only be fixed by his person,
presence, and redeeming work.*
- Paul David Tripp

The Book of Job concludes in chapter 42 with the Lord restoring the fortunes of Job, and we are also told "the Lord gave Job twice as much as he had before" (Job 42:10). The author of the Book of Job then itemizes the things that the Lord gives to Job, including seven sons and three daughters.

"And after this Job lived 140 years, and saw his sons, and his sons' sons, four generations. And Job died, an old man, and full of days" (Job 42:16,17).

Lessons From The Book Of Job

What does the Book of Job teach us? Perhaps, most obviously, *Job teaches us how to suffer in a God-honouring way.* Where others have cursed God, or left the faith altogether, Job continues to call upon God. Job's initial response to the news of what he had lost continues to be one of the most quoted verses from the Old Testament:

"The Lord gave, and the Lord has taken away; blessed be

the name of the Lord" (Job 1:21).

More specifically, *Job teaches us the value of waiting upon the Lord.* If Job's faith comes entirely off the rails—if Job walks away from the Lord—the story ends very differently. Thankfully, Job hangs in there long enough to have a powerful and satisfying encounter with God. While it is true that Job teaches us how to suffer well, and how to be patient in suffering, I do not regard these as the primary lessons from the Book of Job. I'd like to set up what I regard to be the primary value of Job with a quote from Christian philosopher, Peter Kreeft:

> "Job is a mystery. A mystery satisfies something in us, but not our reason. The rationalist is repelled by Job, as Job's three rationalist friends were repelled by Job. But something deeper in us is satisfied by Job, and is nourished…It puts iron in your blood."

My own experience of the Book of Job resonates deeply with Kreeft's words. What is it about Job that is so deeply satisfying? Part of it, I'm sure, is the ultimate vindication of Job and restoration of his fortunes. But more than that, *what is so satisfying about the story of Job is it prepares us for the story of Jesus.* Like every book in the Hebrew Bible, The Book of Job foreshadows the person and experience of Jesus Christ. As Christopher Ash puts it: "(Job) is conspicuously great, exceptionally upright, and definitively righteous. Job in his extremeness foreshadows Jesus in his uniqueness."

~

*What is so satisfying about the story of Job
is it prepares us for the story of Jesus.*

~

As we have noted, Job's suffering is extreme. In the world in which Job lived, righteous living and severe suffering didn't belong together. No one expects a person who is so definitively righteous to suffer so terribly. If God is sovereign—if God controls outcomes—we expect good things to happen to good people and bad things to happen to bad people. And yet, at the heart of human history is the account of Jesus—the most righteous person to have ever lived. And though His accusers could prove no wrong against Him, the rulers of the day crucified Him. Jesus, the greatest man to ever live, suffers terribly and is killed. This counters conventional wisdom. As the apostle Paul explains:

"We preach Christ crucified, a stumbling block to Jews and folly to Gentiles, but to those who are called, both Jews and Greeks, Christ (is) the power of God and the wisdom of God" (1Cor. 1:23,24).

The suffering of Job, the greatest man in the land, is intended to prepare us for the suffering of Jesus, the greatest man in history. I would also suggest that the vindication of Job also foreshadows, in a small way, the vindication of Jesus. Yes, the fortunes that are restored to Job are all temporary—family, wealth, influence and so on. But the hugely relevant point is that the sovereign God of the Universe has the power to work things out in the end. We see this following the death of Jesus, of which Paul writes:

"Therefore God has highly exalted Him and bestowed on Him the name that is above every name, so that at the name of Jesus every knee should bow, in heaven and on earth and under the earth, and every tongue confess that Jesus Christ is Lord, to the glory of God the Father" (Phil. 2:9,10).

Job's vindication prepares us for Jesus' vindication. And Jesus' vindication, in turn, secures our vindication. If you have placed your faith in Jesus Christ—if He is your Lord—then it is my great privilege to declare to you that suffering will not get the final word in your life. A day of vindication awaits you. An eternity of blessing and glory lies ahead.

We are told that, "the Lord gave Job twice as much as he had before" (Job 42:10). I am unable to calculate how much better it will be for us in heaven, but my sense is it will be at least a billion times more than "twice as much". Samuel Rutherford frames the equation well: "One year's time in heaven shall swallow up all sorrows, even beyond all comparison" (Rutherford, *The Loveliness Of Christ*, 29).

The story of Job startles us as we see how vulnerable we are to suffering during our time on earth. But the story of Job also assures us—God is in control, and God will make everything right in the end. The answer you seek will not likely come in the form of an explanation. *God is your answer*. This is the primary lesson of Job.

- Chapter 9 -
The Flames Shall Not Hurt You
Daniel 3:12-30

Christ chargeth me to believe his daylight at midnight.
- Samuel Rutherford

The King of Babylon, Nebuchadnezzar, built a massive golden statue, and commanded the people of the land to worship it. The command to worship the image also included a warning: "whoever does not fall down and worship shall immediately be cast into a burning fiery furnace" (3:6). In other words, nonconformity is grounds for capital punishment. With such a threat looming, we are not surprised to read that when the signal was given, and when the music was sounded, "all the peoples, nations, and languages fell down and worshipped the golden image that King Nebuchadnezzar had set up" (3:7).

Nineteenth century preacher, Charles Spurgeon, in his application of this text, likens our world to Nebuchadnezzar. The culture of our day, like Nebuchadnezzar, expects us to follow its fashions and to obey its rules. The challenge this presents for the Christian is that we must discern how to honour the customs of our land without dishonouring our Lord Jesus Christ. We must learn how to accompany the culture we live in, without accommodating it in an unbiblical manner. Three Jewish men were confronted by this challenge and, in the face of death, chose the honour of God over and against honouring their earthly king.

It would be inaccurate to describe Shadrach, Meshach, and Abednego as "mavericks", or as "renegades". These men had become meaningfully integrated into their culture. We learn in the twelfth verse that these men had been "appointed over the affairs of the province of Babylon". They were willing to serve within the culture, but they were unwilling to conform to a man-made law that would cause them to transgress against God's law. What Nebuchadnezzar required was in clear violation of the first and second Commandments, which read:

"You shall have no other gods before Me. You shall not make for yourself an idol, or any likeness of what is in heaven above or on earth beneath . . . You shall not worship them or serve them; for I, the Lord your God, am a jealous God" (Ex. 20:3-5).

Shadrach, Meshach, and Abednego choose to be faithful to God at a time, and in a manner, that exposes them to the threat of capital punishment. Certain Chaldeans make sure the king hears about Shadrach, Meshach, and Abednego's unwillingness to bow before the image. The three are subsequently summoned to appear before the king and asked:

"Is it true, O Shadrach, Meshach, and Abednego, that you do not serve my gods or worship the golden image that I have set up?" (3:14).

The king then invites the men to make things right by bowing before the image in his presence, and warns that failure to conform will mean death by fire (3:15). What are God's people to do in such a circumstance? We should note three things from the example of Shadrach, Meshach, and Abednego:

1)	*The excuses they could have made*
2)	*The faith they possessed*
3)	*The outcome of their obedience*

Governed By A Concern For God's Glory

First, *the excuses they could have made*. In their deliberations about whether they would conform to this new law, they might have said to themselves: "We are in a foreign land and perhaps we should heed the proverb that says, 'When in Babylon, do as the Babylonians do.'" They might have also reasoned, "We are in public office; we have been trusted to oversee the affairs of this land. We must fulfill our public duty." They could have reasoned with one another, "Everyone else is doing it. It is better to act in accordance with the majority." The legitimate-sounding excuses these men might have accessed were many. We too must guard against transgressing God's law simply because there appears to be some justification, or benefit, in doing so. The sin that is the easiest to linger in is the sin that the majority is steeped in. Shadrach, Meshach, and Abednego held a different perspective. The English Puritan, Thomas Watson, put words to this perspective when he wrote: "It is better to have God approve, than the world applaud."

It has become common in our day to hear: "You don't want to be on the wrong side of history." This kind of statement must never be the measuring stick for the Christian. We are governed by a different principle. We are to be governed by a concern for God and His glory. Accordingly, are you willing to stand alone to do what God has prescribed, and to avoid what He has forbidden?

Unflinching Faith

Having noted the excuses the men could have made, let us note *the faith that these men possessed.* Nebuchadnezzar's question to them is, "who is the god who will deliver you out of my hands?" (3:15). Shadrach, Meshach, and Abednego answer the king:

"Our God whom we serve is able to deliver us from the burning fiery furnace, and he will deliver us out of your hand, O king. But if not, be it known to you, O king, that we will not serve your gods or worship the golden image that you have set up" (3:17, 18).

The faith, and confidence, of these men is manifest in the immediacy of their response. There is no indication that the men hesitated or deliberated. They did not need to huddle together in order to get their responses aligned. Nebuchadnezzar's question, "What god is able to save you?" is met by an unflinching response: "Our God whom we serve is able to deliver us" (3:17).

We should also note that the faith of these men did not hinge on any certainty of being delivered. Their confidence is in God's capacity to save, not in His willingness to save. They do not presume upon God's will and they concede that God may choose not to rescue them. Nevertheless, these men would rather die than disobey God.

Rescue In The Fire

And thirdly, take note of *the outcome of their obedience.* We admit that the immediate outcome was not favourable as the men are bound and thrown into the blazing furnace! But thankfully, the ultimate outcome was immensely positive. The author of Daniel records for us the king's response:

"I see four men unbound, walking in the midst of the fire, and they are not hurt; and the appearance of the fourth is like a son of the gods" (3:25).

Note the unique character of this rescue. Rescue could have come by the Lord causing Nebuchadnezzar to be sympathetic and merciful to the men, but this did not happen. We tend to think of rescue as something that happens before our predicament becomes too dire or desperate. But that's not what we see here. Indeed, the Lord often ordains to rescue *in* the fire rather than *from* the fire. Rather than hedge us from all adversity and discomfort, God uses the furnace of challenging circumstances to make us more like His Son. Our hymn, *How Firm A Foundation*, captures this well:

When through fiery trials thy pathway shall lie,
My grace, all-sufficient, shall be thy supply:
The flames shall not hurt thee; I only design
Thy dross to consume, and thy gold to refine.

~
The Lord often ordains to rescue in the fire rather than from the fire.
~

The Fourth Man

I get chills as I think about the presence of the "fourth man" in the furnace with Shadrach, Meshach, and Abednego. The king notices the countenance of the fourth man is different, and describes his appearance by saying, "(he) is like a son of the gods". I agree with those biblical commentators who see "the fourth man" as an Incarnation of God (or, Pre-Incarnate Christ). This is consistent with the character of the God revealed in the Scriptures. That God would show up in person to rescue His people from grave danger. Indeed, God's way of rescuing is neither impersonal nor remote.

When the furnace of difficult circumstances in your life is turned up, you should be looking for the abiding care of "the fourth man", Jesus Christ. You may not see Him with your eyes like the men in today's passage, but the presence of "the fourth man", Jesus Christ, may be no less real and profound. Has this been your experience? Bring to your mind your most painful moments, and ask yourself: "Where was Jesus during my season of pain and grief?"

I want to share something deeply personal with the hope that it may help some of you see "the fourth man" at work in your particular situation. A dear colleague of mine helped me to detect the "fourth man's" presence as I shared with him my experience of officiating at my sister's funeral in 2019. During the funeral service, and during the graveside service, I had a pretty good lid on my emotions, because that's the way I was raised. In my family, you keep a "stiff upper lip". Crying and public displays of grief are discouraged. Perhaps you were raised in a family like that.

I am standing next to my sister's casket at the graveside acting as though everything is under control. But on the inside I was a mess. I was hurting badly. It was one of the hardest days of my entire life. As soon as I finished the Benediction at the graveside, I immediately retreated on foot knowing I couldn't keep my emotions together a minute longer. I quickly walked through the cemetery knowing that, about 50-60 yards away, was where my mom and dad were buried. I was determined to grieve privately at the grave of my parents, but something in my spirit made me turn around when I was almost there. My daughter, Anya, was following me, about ten yards behind. My wife, Allie, was a few yards behind her. Allie's parents were heading in my direction too. In one of the most painful moments of my life "the fourth man" sent four people to chase me down.

Just seeing them come after me was enough. My mind still has a very clear picture of what I saw in that moment. Whether they realized it or not, they were Incarnating God's loving care for me, and it was the most comforting thing I have ever experienced in my life.

"Yea, though I walk through the valley of the shadow of death, I fear no evil. For Thou art with me; Thy rod and Thy staff, they comfort me" (Ps. 23:4).

It's often the case that the Lord's "rod" and "staff" are the Lord's people. Be on the look out and I'm confident that you'll see the "fourth man" show up in your life through His people. The Lord does not need to part the sea, or shut the mouths of lions, in order to rescue you. He may use means that appear quite ordinary on the surface. One way or another, the Lord Jesus Christ will abide with you. One way or another, Jesus Christ will comfort and strengthen you.

- Chapter 10 -
What Your Troubles Achieve
2 Corinthians 4:8-18

It is our duty and glory to not measure afflictions by the smart but by the end.
- Thomas Brooks

We gain assurance from the apostle Paul in 2 Corinthians 4 that our suffering is not in vain. The testimony of the apostle Paul is that, for the Christian, a positive outcome will ultimately emerge from our troubles. Paul was familiar with adversity and pain. The list of Paul's afflictions provided in 2 Corinthians 11 is staggering:

Paul's Resume Of Suffering

"Beaten times without number, often in danger of death. Five times I received from the Jews 39 lashes. Three times I was beaten with rods, once I was stoned, three times I was shipwrecked, a night and day I have spent in the deep. I have been on frequent journeys, in dangers from rivers, dangers from robbers, dangers from my countrymen, dangers from the Gentiles, dangers in the city, dangers in the wilderness, dangers on the sea, dangers among the false brethren; I have been in labour and hardship, through many sleepless nights, in hunger and thirst, often without food, in cold and exposure" (2Cor. 11:24-27).

In spite of all of these hardships, Paul brings forward *a message of hope*. He puts it this way:

> *"We are hard pressed on every side, but not crushed; perplexed, but not in despair; persecuted, but not abandoned; struck down, but not destroyed"* (2Cor. 4:8-9).

Using these parallel paradoxes, Paul repeats the common motif of this letter: *weakness invites strength*. More precisely, *our weakness—our troubles—invite God's presence and provision.* At no point do you hear Paul talk about "looking within", or "digging deep", or "sucking it up". He knew that he didn't have it within himself to carry on, but he was certain that God would provide support sufficient for the trial. Paul also understood that his troubles were achieving something immensely positive. He even describes his troubles as "momentary" and "light" in 4:17.

How can Paul say that? How could *anyone* ever say that? If you take a minute to think about what you've been through—or what you're currently going through, you wouldn't call that suffering "light", would you? Some of you know what it is like to suffer deeply with something for decades—you wouldn't describe your suffering as "momentary", would you? So, how does Paul do it?

Measuring Suffering With The Correct Scale

Paul regards his intense, ongoing, suffering as "light and momentary" *by comparing it with something.* Our first clue is found in 4:13-14, where Paul says he is approaching his suffering with a "spirit of faith". "Spirit of faith" in what, Paul? Faith in yourself? Faith in God's imminent deliverance? Faith in a cloud with a silver lining? No. The object of Paul's faith is found in verse 14—Paul's faith in face of suffering is based on his conviction that "He who raised the Lord Jesus will raise us also with Jesus."

Paul is able to endure his present suffering by focusing on future glory. "Therefore", he says (because we will one day be raised with Jesus), "we do not lose heart, but though our outer man is decaying, yet our inner man is being renewed day by day" (2Cor. 4:16). Paul is not blind to his suffering. This is not some "mind over matter" trick he is advocating. Paul recognizes that his body is "decaying". He knows, as we do, that suffering is unpleasant. Christians are not expected to pretend that it doesn't hurt. What Paul does expect, however, is that our lives demonstrate the comforting truth that suffering does not get the last word. In Romans 8:18, Paul declares:

"the sufferings of this present time are not worthy to be compared with the glory that is to be revealed to us."

The Puritan, Thomas Watson, reminds us, "Affliction may be lasting, but it is not everlasting." The reality, however, is that when we are suffering it seems like forever. And this is precisely why we need Paul's perspective. Our suffering is but a small piece within a much larger fabric. As Paul puts it:

"our light and momentary troubles are achieving for us an eternal glory that far outweighs them all" (2Cor. 4:17).

Now—again—when Paul says that our affliction is "momentary", he does not mean that it lasts for only fifteen minutes. When he says that our suffering is "momentary", he means that it only lasts a lifetime. And a lifetime, of course, is only "momentary" when we compare it with eternity. Paul understood that his afflictions would not outlive this present life. Paul did not lose heart because he looked forward to a time when his afflictions would come to an end—permanently.

Not only does Paul consider his afflictions to be "momentary", but we also see that he refers to them as being "light". Come on, Paul, your afflictions were hardly "light"! You have been imprisoned, beaten up, stoned, shipwrecked, hungry, exposed—how can you say that your affliction is "light"? When Paul says that his afflictions are "light", he does not mean that they are easy or painless. He means that compared to what is coming they are as nothing. To consider suffering "light" one must compare it to the "eternal weight of glory". Compared to the coming "weight of glory", our afflictions are like feathers in the scale.

Thinking Deeply About Heaven

In our day and age, Christians who are serious about their contemplation of heaven are often ridiculed and accused of having their "heads in the clouds". And yet, Paul actually encourages an ongoing contemplation of heaven. In Colossians 3:2, Paul commands us: "Set your mind on the things above, not on the things that are on earth." The Eighteenth century Scottish theologian, Thomas Boston, asserts the same: "Had we a clearer view of the other world, we should not make so much of either the smiles or frowns of this" (Boston, *The Crook In The Lot*, 107). One of the primary ways we endure amid adversity is through a careful contemplation of heaven.

Paul, like any of us, felt the sting and pressure of suffering, but when he compared his sufferings to that future blessedness awaiting him in heaven something changed. It caused him to say to the Philippians, "to live is Christ and to die is gain…I desire to depart and be with Christ, which is better by far" (Phil. 1:21,23). And, as John Calvin comments, "(Contemplating heaven) makes light that which previously seemed heavy, and makes brief and momentary that which seemed of boundless duration." Dear reader, serious contemplation of heaven's glory is an essential Christian discipline.

Inward Renovation

While thinking deeply about heaven is vital, Paul also points to a more immediate benefit that emerges from our suffering:

"Though our outer man is decaying, yet our inner man is being renewed day by day" (2Cor. 4:16).

Paul starts with something bad—our outer decay—but he ends with something good—the renewal of "our inner man". Paul goes on to say that our "troubles are achieving for us an eternal weight of glory" (2Cor. 4:17). The Bible is clear on this point: in the midst of our suffering, something good is taking place. Our challenge, of course, is that "the decay is visible, and the renovation is invisible" (Calvin).

If we were given a choice in the matter, my guess is that none of us would choose to suffer. I include myself in that statement. And while none of us would choose to suffer, we should not lose sight of the blessed thing that suffering produces. Samuel Rutherford said that when he was cast into "the cellars of affliction", he remembered, "the great King always kept his wine there". Similarly, Charles Spurgeon remarks, "those who dive in the sea of affliction always bring up rare pearls."

If we are ever to regard our suffering as momentary, if we are to ever regard our suffering as light, we must always have in view the rare pearls God intends to uncover for us. We must always have in view the choice wine God intends to serve to us. We must always have in view the infinite value of our eternal relationship with Jesus Christ.

There is much for the follower of Christ to gain from suffering. Suffering shapes us in a way that prosperity never can. It's mind-bending in a way. We love prosperity and we pursue comforts every single day. We hate suffering and we resist it at every turn. And yet, God has so ordered things that we achieve far more from our suffering than we ever do from our prosperity.

God will not waste your suffering. Consider often what our troubles are achieving. Our Lord assures us that something good and glorious is emerging from our troubles. May we learn to pray as Samuel Rutherford did:

"Lord cut, Lord carve, Lord wound, Lord do anything that may perfect thy Father's image in us, and make us meet* for glory" (Rutherford, *The Loveliness Of Christ*, 7) *

> ~
> *God has so ordered things that we achieve far more from our suffering than we ever do from our prosperity.*
> ~

*fit.

- Chapter 11 -
God's Provision For The Downcast
2 Corinthians 7:4-7

*There is no sweeter fellowship with Christ than
to bring our wounds and our sores to Him.
- Samuel Rutherford*

None of us is immune to sorrow. And even the sincerest of Christians experience seasons of sadness. This was certainly the case with the apostle Paul. But the great encouragement we gain from observing Paul comes when we note that he didn't remain "downcast". God intervened—God brought real comfort to Paul in his time of trouble.

The ESV translates the Greek as "downcast" in 7:6. The KJV translates similarly to, "those who are cast down". The New American Standard translates the word as "depressed". The Greek literally means, "to be brought low"—presumably by external pressures. Paul's not talking about occasional bouts with melancholy here. He is not talking about having an "off day". He is talking about an experience of pain and suffering that has literally brought him to his knees.

As I reflect on the most painful moments of my life, they all had this in common—they didn't simply bring me low emotionally, they also brought me low physically. When our sadness is acute, almost instinctively, we go to the floor—or we go facedown in our bed. Perhaps you know what it is like for sadness to deliver a knockout blow. Paul certainly did. But Paul got up again. And because Paul found such profound encouragement amid his suffering, his testimony should command our full attention.

Transparency Amid Pain

The tone of Paul's testimony is surprisingly positive when we read verse 4. He says, "I am greatly encouraged; in all our troubles my joy knows no bounds." First, let us note that Paul is not in denial about his troubles. He does not engage in a kind of mental trickery where he imagines that everything is fine when it really isn't. Again, he says, "*in all our troubles* my joy knows no bounds." Unless we are familiar with "all" that Paul has been through we risk missing the impact of this statement. Paul has been repeatedly beaten up; he's been repeatedly whipped; he's been stoned and left for dead; he's been shipwrecked; he's been imprisoned; he's harmed by foreigners and betrayed by fellow countrymen—and the list goes on. Paul describes his troubles further in 7:5:

> *"When we came to Macedonia, this body of ours had no rest, but we were harassed at every turn—conflicts on the outside, fears within."*

Here we see that Paul's troubles are not limited to what is happening *to* him, but they extend to what is happening *in* him. That's what severe trials do, don't they? In some cases, the physical harm is less severe than the mental and emotional anguish, which follows and lingers. It seems that there is no aspect of suffering that Paul hasn't experienced—and yet, he nevertheless declares that "(he) is greatly encouraged" and that "in all (his) troubles (his) joy knows no bounds."

How did Paul get here? Where did he find this encouragement amid such hardship? Paul's answer is that he gained encouragement and joy from the Lord. Before we write off such a response as being trite or simplistic, let's look precisely at what he says:

"we were harassed at every turn—conflicts on the outside, fears within. But God, who comforts the downcast, comforted us by the coming of Titus" (2Cor. 7:5,6).

A Practical, Divinely Given, Remedy

Paul gives both a theological answer and a practical answer, and the two are inseparable. The theological remedy is that Paul belongs to a "God who comforts the downcast." And the practical remedy is that Titus shows up! As Paul discerns it, God had come to him through Titus' arrival. As Paul discerns it, God had sent His encouragement through a human being. When we hurt—when sadness overcomes us and brings us low—God has an immensely practical remedy for His children. God provides His hurting children with a "Titus." In other words, God provides Spirit-filled individuals who have the capacity to incarnate His comfort for us.

Philip Yancey, in his popular volume, "Where Is God When It Hurts?" answers his question by asking another question: "Where is *the Church* when it hurts?" Yancey asks this second question understanding that the Church is the means by which a spiritual God intends to function within a physical environment. Just as God comforted Paul by the coming of Titus, He intends to comfort you and me through the provision of our Christian friends.

*God provides Spirit-filled individuals who have
the capacity to incarnate His comfort for us.*

I fear that very few Christians take advantage of this principle. I am struck by how common it is for followers of Jesus to avoid Christian fellowship when they are in pain. My experience has been that people are more likely to come to church when all is well, and when the seas of life are calm. But when things begin to fall apart—when the storms of life descend, many react by staying away from church. If we do this we miss out on God's ordained means for comfort.

Don't Hide From Other Christians

Based on what we learn from the apostle Paul, suffering should drive us to seek out Christian fellowship; it should drive us to seek out a "Titus"—it should drive us to seek out Christians who can incarnate God's comfort for us. Indeed, it is important to note that Paul was actually looking for Titus. He was not moping. He was not resigning himself to a life of pain, but rather, he actively sought after encouragement and comfort. To see this, we have to flip back to the second chapter, verses 12 and 13, where Paul writes:

"Now when I went to Troas . . . I still had no peace of mind, because I did not find my brother Titus there. So I said goodbye to them and went on to Macedonia."

Do you see Paul's determination here? Paul's hurting. He's looking for Titus in Troas, but Titus isn't there. So he keeps going. He's off to Macedonia. Paul doesn't settle down and he doesn't give up until he finds Titus. Part of me wishes that obtaining God's comfort were more automatic than this. Part of me wishes that gaining comfort were easier. And because obtaining comfort isn't automatic, we need to follow Paul's example and *seek Christian fellowship.*

God does not intend for us to face suffering alone. God purposes to always be with us. And, quite practically, God often purposes to be with us by sending us a Christian brother or sister. "God, who comforts the downcast, comforted (Paul) by the coming of Titus."

At this point, we may be curious to ask, "What exactly did Titus *do,* or what did Titus *say,* that brought such comfort to Paul?" It is interesting to see that Paul does not mention a single thing that Titus *said*—not a word is recorded for our benefit. Nor is anything written about what Titus *did* for Paul. Paul simply acknowledges his timely arrival. I think Philip Yancey has it right: "It is not our words or our insights that (hurting people) want most; it is our mere presence" (Yancey, *Where Is God When It Hurts?,* 177). Perhaps your own experience confirms this. Mine does.

As I reflect upon those painful moments in my life, I can immediately bring to mind those individuals who stood with me. Curiously, I cannot recall what any of them said. I only recall that they stood with me, and that was enough to supply me with great comfort.

Find Your Place In The Hospital

It has already been suggested that all of us will experience suffering in this life. No one is exempt. But, for some, your season of suffering might not be the present. You may be currently enjoying a season of ease and prosperity. Perhaps you are thinking, "Well, this is an encouraging passage—it is nice to know that God cares, but I am doing quite fine. I'm sorry about all of the troubles that Paul had to endure, but that is not my experience." If that is you—if life is good for you—there remains for you a necessary application: You must seek to be a "Titus" for hurting Christian brothers and sisters.

The Christian Church has sometimes been described as a hospital (J.I. Packer). I think this is a helpful analogy. Not all of us are well. Some of us have been severely wounded. But some of us are well and are equipped to help others. Some of us enter Christian fellowship as *patients* and some of us come as *nurses*. Some of us come as *a hurting Paul* and some of us come as *a helping Titus*.

If you are a "Paul" you ought neither to conceal your wounds, nor avoid Christian fellowship. And if you are a "Titus" you must not neglect seeking out those who need your encouragement and support. Remember how this turns out as Paul and Titus come together. Paul moves from despair to encouragement, and even amid great challenges he declares, "my joy knows no bounds" (7:4).

God has made adequate provision for those who hurt. You may be downcast—you may have been knocked down by the challenges in your life. But God intends to pick you back up again. Engage in Christian fellowship and look for your "Titus" there.

- Chapter 12 -
Gladly Weak
2 Corinthians 12:7-10

*Out of the bitterest drug God distils His glory,
and our happiness.
- Thomas Watson*

The apostle Paul begins 2 Corinthians 12 by boasting. Paul is responding to comparisons being made between his "no frills" approach to ministry and the outwardly impressive ministry of some of his colleagues. Just when it appears that Paul is going to finally unpack his impressive spiritual resume, he pivots and declares: "I will not boast, except of my weaknesses" (2Cor. 12:5).

"Now, Paul, that is a strange thing to say. We're not asking you to be a showoff. We just want to know that you've had some successes in ministry." Paul's statement does seem a bit unusual at first, doesn't it? "I will not boast, except of my weaknesses"?

I can assure you that when the St. Andrew's Kirk search committee flew me down to Nassau, Bahamas in January of 2010 for an interview, I did not follow Paul's lead on this. I did not say to the search committee, "Why don't we all take my resume and put it through the shredder. I really don't feel comfortable sharing with you anything that I've accomplished; I just want you to know about my *weaknesses*. I want to spend the rest of this interview boasting about *what is lacking* in me." Can you imagine? How do we make sense of what Paul is saying? Charles Spurgeon calls the "when" and "then" of verse 10 the "hinges upon which (the text) turns." Paul writes, "For *when* I am weak, *then* I am strong" (2Cor. 12:10)

Power From Weakness

What does this mean? It means when the Christian is consciously weak, *when* we are acutely aware of our inability to remedy our most challenging predicaments; it is *then* we are positioned to be strong. In reality, we are always weak. As finite, fallen, human beings, we are always lacking—whether we are willing to admit this or not. This is what the Bible tells us. Jesus says, "apart from Me you can do nothing" (Jn. 15:5). And yet, *when* we embrace our limitations, and *when* we confess our weaknesses to God and plead for His assistance, *then* we are strong in His might.

The grand lesson that Paul learns is that pain and suffering and weakness invites God's strength. This is why Paul can say, "Therefore I will boast all the more gladly of my weaknesses, so that the power of Christ may rest upon me" (12:9). The notion that God's strength emerges from human weakness is a thread, which runs through this entire letter. You might also say that this same thread runs through the Gospel itself. As one commentator puts it, "power in weakness is shorthand for the gospel. In God's plan of redemption, there had to be weakness (crucifixion) before there was power (resurrection)" (Hughes, *2 Corinthians*, 214).

The consistent testimony of Scripture confirms God's interest in helping those who are most vulnerable. Or, as Spurgeon puts it, "God helps us most when we most need His help." We read about Paul's life experiences and it's impossible to miss how frequently he is in need of God's assistance. It is also evident that, like us, Paul is eager to gain relief from his suffering. He is not indifferent about his pain. He likens his suffering to having a "thorn in (his) flesh" and is desperate to have it removed (2 Cor. 12:7). Paul dislikes this particular hardship so much that he prays three times for God to remove it.

When Pain Lingers

Paul wants relief, and yet, he also detects God's purposes at work amid his adversity. He senses that his suffering is helping to keep him grounded, and humble (2 Cor. 12:7). Understanding this principle led Thomas Boston to assert, "It is far more needful for us to have our spirits humbled under (adversity), than to have the (adversity) removed" (Boston, *The Crook In The Lot*, 84).

Paul also identifies Satan as having a role to play in his suffering. He discerns how the enemy wishes to torment him with this adversity, which heightens his desire for relief and prompts his prayers to God. And while God responds favourably to Paul's prayers, He doesn't remove the thorn. This is our clue that there is a Divine purpose behind our pain. If our pain remains, if our trial lingers, if we feel like our prayers for rescue are falling on "deaf ears", it is likely because our suffering has not yet produced its intended result.

The Benefits Of Suffering

This is not to say that suffering is good. It's not. We do not *court* suffering. We do not *like* suffering. And yet, what the Christ-follower ought to embrace is that which our suffering produces. As many Christians have recognized, what God does in us through suffering is usually far more profound than what He does in us through prosperity. Have you ever heard anyone say, "The most satisfying periods of growth in my life have come during times of extended ease and comfort"? Nobody says that. It isn't true. What's true is described by Charles Spurgeon:

"I am afraid that all the grace that I have got of my comfortable and easy times and happy hours, might almost lie on a penny. But the good that I have received from my sorrows, and pains, and griefs, is altogether incalculable."

> ~
> *What the Christ-follower ought to embrace*
> *is that which our suffering produces.*
> ~

Basic physiology tells us that if you want a muscle to grow, you need to agitate it. If you want to lose muscle, go sit on your sofa all day and watch sports, or Netflix, or whatever it is which attracts you to such inactivity. Increased muscle size, muscle strength, and muscle density is the result of constantly agitating your muscles with heavy weight and then feeding your body protein during the recovery. Similarly, God allows us to be agitated—not because He is unkind, but because He desires our growth. God permits us to struggle in order to strengthen us by the struggle, and then He nurtures us during the recovery period.

Paul learned that he wasn't on his own when he suffered, and that God was sustaining and strengthening him during seasons of pain. We would do well to recognize the same. What God speaks to Paul, is also true for us:

"My grace is sufficient for you, for my power is made perfect in weakness"(2Cor. 12:9)

When God calls His grace "sufficient", He is saying that it is enough. Moreover, God is saying that *He* is enough.

- Chapter 13 -
Joy And Pain
James 1:1-12

*In our suffering God is at work to give us
something much better than what we want.*
- Paul David Tripp

J̶ames writes his letter in order to encourage Jewish believers living in challenging conditions. In James' day, like in our day, many profess to have a faith in Christ without living in a manner that demonstrates a genuine possessing of faith. The very first marker that James establishes to verify genuine faith is how we respond to trials. Admittedly, it is a challenging standard that is presented:

"Count it all joy, my brothers, when you meet trials of various kinds" (Jas. 1:2).

The Certainty Of Trials

Before we attempt to determine how we can have joy amid serious trials, it will be important to note some things about the trials referenced by James. Firstly, note *the certainty of trials in a person's life*. I think it is with great purpose that James says, *"when* you meet trials" rather than *"if* you face trials". I worry that some Christians believe that their relationship with Christ will insulate them from the problems of this world. But I do not see the Scriptures supporting this view. What we do see are biblical authors, like James, preparing us for the inevitability of hardship and adversity.

The Variety Of Trials

Secondly, James wants us to note *the variety of trials in a person's life*. James says we will "meet trials of *various* kinds". The Greek could also be translated as "multicoloured". In other words, *not every trial is alike*. As Pastor Alistair Begg puts it, "Some trials are the common lot of our imperfect existence." Because we are fallen creatures, living in a fallen world, some bad things are going to happen—accidents, sickness, and so on. Begg points this out in order to make a distinction between "the trials that we *meet* and the trials that we *make*". Some of us have had the experience of trials that were of our own making. We've made certain decisions that weren't particularly wise and, as a result, various trials followed.

Joy From Pain

Once we understand that *trials are a certainty*, and that there are a *variety of trials* we might potentially face, we are left with this immensely challenging *exhortation to experience joy in the midst of our trials*. It hardly needs to be said that this exhortation is calling for a response that is entirely unnatural for us. When I think about how to get joy, I don't normally think about what kind of trouble I can get into. I don't say to myself, "What kind of hardship can I subject myself to in order to maximize my joy?" No! The opposite is true. We spend our resources and our energy in an attempt to *avoid* hardship, don't we? We imagine that if we can succeed in diminishing, or eliminating, every kind of opposition or hardship, then our life will be joyful.

Tim Keller notes the same, while highlighting the futility of pursuing a life free from hardship:

> "No matter what precautions we take, no matter how well we have put together a good life, no matter how hard we have worked to be healthy, wealthy, comfortable with friends and family, and successful in our career—something will inevitably ruin it. No amount of money, power, and planning can prevent bereavement, dire illness, relationship betrayal, financial disaster, or a host of other troubles from entering your life" (Keller, *Walking With God Through Pain And Suffering*, 3).

The inevitability of suffering, and its variety of trials, might discourage us if it wasn't for the benefits we gain from them. Indeed, James asserts that *amid trials there are great benefits to be uncovered.*

> *"Count it all joy, my brothers, when you meet trials of various kinds, for you know that the testing of your faith produces steadfastness. And let steadfastness have its full effect, that you may be perfect and complete, lacking in nothing"* (Jas. 1:2-4).

We must be careful to note what James is *not* saying. James does not say, "Count it all joy, my brothers, when you meet trials because your trials aren't nearly as bad as you think they are." Nor does James say, "Count it all joy, my brothers, when you meet trials because trials should be enjoyed." No, we're not going to enjoy the trial. As the author of Hebrews admits, "No discipline seems pleasant at the time, but painful" (Heb. 12:11). Your trials aren't going to fill you with joy. Your trials are more likely to fill you with sadness and pain. And yet, James calls us to rejoice in what our suffering is producing.

Trials As God's Pencil

By facing and overcoming pain, fear, and anxiety, we move to a better state than if we had never experienced these things in the first place. Trials can be awful, but when managed by a God who is sovereign and kind, trials can serve to make us more like Christ—and that's the part we rejoice in. The English Puritan, Thomas Watson, puts it well:

"God's rod is a pencil to draw Christ's image more distinctly upon us" (Watson, *Gleanings*, 141).

> ~
> *Trials can be awful, but when managed by*
> *a God who is sovereign and kind, trials*
> *can serve to make us more like Christ.*
> ~

Our faith will not grow to its full potential unless it be tried and tested by the challenges that adversity brings. Alistair Begg makes the analogy of boiling an egg. You put the egg under the extreme pressure of boiling water and, after a certain amount of time, you have a hard-boiled egg that you can peel and eat. However, if you take the egg out of the boiling water too soon you will have a big mess on your hands. This analogy is helpful for those of us who are desperate to get out of the hot water we are in. The trial is uncomfortable and we want out. We're looking for the exit and we want to make a run for it.

James reminds us how trials test our faith and help to develop "steadfastness". James charges us to "let steadfastness have its full effect, that you may be perfect and complete, lacking in nothing" (Jas. 1:4). I may not like the pressure of being in boiling water, but if escaping the pressure prematurely makes a big mess, then leave me in until the work is done.

Consider God's purposes as you endure hardship. Be mindful of His design to make you more like Christ. And count it pure joy!

- Chapter 14 -
Jesus' Concern For Your Pain
John 11:17-44

*It is said of God that no one can behold his face and live. I al-
ways thought this meant that no one could see his splendor and
live. A friend said perhaps it means that no one could see his
sorrow and live. Or perhaps his sorrow is his splendor.*
– Nicholas Wolterstorff

*Sermon preached on September 8, 2019—one week after
Hurricane Dorian devastated the Northern Bahamas.*

Can I be certain of God's concern for my pain? What about
the people of Abaco and Grand Bahama? God, in His sovereignty, has allowed a Category 5 Hurricane to hit our
Northern islands. Precious souls have perished. Almost everyone I speak to has a loved one in either Abaco or Grand Bahama,
and their lives have been turned upside down. Thousands upon
thousands have been displaced from their homes. Some may
never be able to return. And no matter how much of the news
we watch, no matter how much we see on social media, it is still
difficult to wrap our minds around what has transpired, and the
level of devastation, which has resulted.

*Can we be certain of God's concern for the people of
the Northern Bahamas?* I don't want us to answer this question
emotionally, or even instinctively. God has spoken to us in His
Word, and so we look to His Word for an answer to our ques-

tion. In John 11, one of Jesus' friends, Lazarus of Bethany, had become ill, and so Martha and Mary (the sisters of Lazarus) sent word to Jesus about the condition of their brother (Jn. 11:1-3).

When Jesus Delays His Response

The reader is likely shocked—or, at least, surprised to read that when Jesus hears that His friend is unwell he remains where He is for two more days (11:6). And just so we don't misinterpret Jesus' delay as indifference, the apostle John tells us, "Jesus loved Martha and her sister and Lazarus" (Jn. 11:5). So, we have this dire situation, and Martha and Mary call for Jesus—their friend—and He doesn't come…At least not right away.

Many of us have had similar experiences. An important relationship is falling apart. We're struggling to make ends meet. Our physical health is failing. A loved one is suffering, and so we call out to Jesus. We ask Jesus to come and intercede on our behalf. But He delays His coming. *Hurricane Dorian* begins to descend upon The Bahamas and we call out to Jesus. We petition the One who created the stars and calls them by name, and we ask Him to swing the Hurricane out to sea. Days later, with Hurricane Dorian sitting on Grand Bahama, we call out to the One who controls the wind and the waves and we beg God to just move the storm forward—even just a little bit! But He delays His coming. *Can we be certain of God's concern for our pain and suffering?*

Lazarus was gravely ill. Jesus delays His coming and Lazarus dies. Martha goes out to greet Jesus, and she says:

"Lord, if You had been here, my brother would not have died" (Jn. 11:21).

Some of us have wondered the same.

> "Lord, if you had been here, my marriage would not have fallen apart."
> "Lord, if you had been here, my loved one would not have died."
> "Lord, if you had been here this terrible thing would not have happened."

Martha's perspective is that Jesus is too late. We sometimes think that as well, don't we? As we consider the devastation in the Northern Bahamas, some of us are thinking that right now. Even still, Jesus greets Martha with a gracious reply in verse 23: "Your brother will rise again." Martha's perspective, however, remains limited. She can't seem to get past her conviction that the opportunity to heal Lazarus has gone. "I know that he will rise again in the resurrection on the last day", she says (Jn. 11:24). We see a measure of faith in Martha's response, but her faith is tempered by her view of reality.

A Call To Faith

That's often our challenge, isn't it? In attempting to be guided by reasonable expectations, we run the danger of settling for less than what is possible if Jesus were to apply His power. We possess a measure of faith in Jesus, but our view of what Jesus will do for us is often quite small. And then, like Martha, we have our limited notions shattered by Jesus, who says, "I am the Resurrection and the life. Whoever believes in Me, though he die, yet shall he live" (Jn. 11:25). This statement is staggering in the best sort of way. Jesus declares that He possesses authority over life and death. "Do you believe this?" He asks Martha (Jn.

11:26). "Do you believe I am who I say I am, and do you believe that I possess the power to bestow life in the face of death?"

I could not do what I do as a pastor, if there is no Resurrection. I have officiated at hundreds of funerals over the last twenty years. These funerals have included children, members of my own family, and persons who suffered terribly.

Precious souls have perished in Abaco and Grand Bahama. Children are numbered among them. In such times we may feel the temptation to say, "Lord, if you were here this would not have happened." But the Christian must resist this temptation. We resist this because we affirm that Jesus is the Son of God, the Saviour from sin, and has ultimately defeated death. And so the Christian grieves differently. The Christian grieves the temporary loss, because of what Jesus has promised:

"I am the Resurrection and the life. Whoever believes in Me, though he die, yet shall he live" (Jn. 11:25).

Do you believe this?

Emotional Jesus

To help Martha's faith, and ours, Jesus provides a foretaste of the Resurrection. Jesus had determined to bring Lazarus, four days in the grave, back from the dead (Jn. 11:39). Jesus determined that God would be most glorified—not in the prevention of suffering, but in the triumph over suffering (Jn. 11:4). But before He does that, we see Jesus respond to death in a very human way:

"When Jesus saw (Mary) weeping, and the Jews who had come with her also weeping, he was deeply moved in his

spirit and greatly troubled. And he said, "Where have you laid him?" They said to him, "Lord, come and see." Jesus wept" (Jn. 11:33-35).

There are not enough words on this earth to describe the profundity of these two words together: *Jesus wept.*

The eternal Son of God; the Creator of the Universe; the Saviour of the world—*weeping* at the grave of a friend. Remember, this is the One who has authority over life and death. Jesus knows that, in just a few moments, He will bring Lazarus back to life. And yet, at the sight of His friend's tomb…With the smell of death overwhelming them…In the presence of grieving friends….*Jesus weeps.*

Jesus understands the ugliness of death. The Son of God experiences grief. The pain of His friends matters immensely to Jesus. *Can we be certain of God's concern for our pain? Yes we can!*

Death's Conqueror

I wonder if there was more going on in the heart and mind of Jesus than just the death of His friend Lazarus. The Son of God came to earth because the human race has fallen badly from our original design. Not only have the effects of sin marred us, but also the earth itself has become marred and groans for renewal. Disease and disaster were not a part of the original plan. Sickness, sorrow, grief, suffering—these are signals that we are not yet where we ultimately are supposed to be. Jesus came to set us on a new trajectory and as a demonstration of His power over death, and as a foretaste of His own Resurrection, Jesus shouted with a loud voice:

"'Lazarus, come out.' (And) the man who had died came out" (Jn. 11:43-44).

The grand point of this account is quite straightforward. *Jesus can be trusted.* Jesus can be trusted with your life, and all of its complexities. Jesus can even be trusted with your death. His promise is to go and prepare a place for you, so that where He is, you may be also (Jn. 14:1-6).

You have regularly heard me quote, what I think is an old Puritan proverb:

When we cannot trace the providence of God, we must trust His character.

> ~
> *Jesus can be trusted with your life, and all of its complexities. Jesus can even be trusted with your death.*
> ~

We do not know precisely why we have suffered the way we have. I cannot tell you why *Hurricane Dorian* inflicted the terrible damage that it did. But I do know this: God is good, and His intentions are kind. His steadfast love endures forever, and His mercies are new every morning. God can be trusted. When we cannot trace the providence of God, we can trust His character. God is concerned with your pain and with mine. As the psalmist declares:

"The Lord is near to the brokenhearted and saves the crushed in spirit" (Ps. 34:18).

Our Lord Jesus is indeed near. Jesus wept, and *Jesus weeps with His people*. Until *that day* when He promises to wipe our tears away, and pain, and suffering, and death are no more. Do you believe this? Jesus can be trusted.

Chapter 15

A Mighty Fortress Is Our God
Psalm 46

The sovereignty of God is the pillow upon which the Christian rests their head.
- Charles Spurgeon

Sermon preached on September 22, 2019—three weeks after Hurricane Dorian devastated the Northern Bahamas.

It has been three weeks since Hurricane Dorian tore through the Northern Bahamas. Even three weeks later it remains difficult for us to measure the full extent of the devastation. We're still not sure how many people perished in the storm. There are over 1,000 persons still unaccounted for. Thousands of homes have been destroyed. Tens of thousands of people have been displaced. For most of those who were forced to leave their homes, life will never be the same.

Vulnerability Exposed

It is a massive understatement for me to say that this storm has made us feel very vulnerable. And yet, even as I say that, I'm mindful that the Bible consistently teaches that vulnerability is our natural condition as human beings. If that's the case, hardships don't simply make us vulnerable, but they reveal our pre-existing vulnerability. This was C.S. Lewis' discovery following the death of his wife:

"God has not been trying an experiment on my faith or love in order to find out their quality. He knew it already. It was I who didn't…He always knew that my temple was a house of cards. His only way of making me realize the fact was to knock it down" (Lewis, *A Grief Observed*, 52).

The apostle Peter describes our vulnerability, quoting the prophet Isaiah: "All flesh is like grass and all its glory like the flower of grass" (1Pet. 1:24). We read that and we wonder, "In what way are human beings like grass, or like the flower of the grass?" Peter answers: "The grass withers, and the flower falls" (1Pet. 1:24). That's a pretty sobering image, isn't it? James ratchets things up even further when he writes, "What is your life? For you are a mist that appears for a little time and then vanishes" (Jas. 4:14).

Hardships don't simply make us vulnerable, but they reveal our pre-existing vulnerability. Intrinsically we know this, and so we spend much of our energy and resources in an effort to make us less vulnerable. This can be something as simple as locking our doors, to wearing a seatbelt, to keeping our money in a bank. Most businesses in Nassau hire security guards (St. Andrew's Kirk hires security guards!) because we want to be less vulnerable. The reason why many of us go to work each week is related to our security. We imagine if we make enough money, it will help us survive the day of trial. Not only do we sense our vulnerability as it relates to forces outside of us, but our aging bodies remind us that our body is fragile and vulnerable. Some of us work very hard to make our body a little less fragile. We eat healthy foods (not me, other people). We exercise in an effort to strengthen our body. If we get sick, we immediately seek remedies to restore our body's health.

~
Hardships don't simply make us vulnerable,
but they reveal our pre-existing vulnerability.
~

I don't want to discourage you from any of this. Wear a seatbelt. Lock your door at night. Be diligent in your employment. Eat a salad. Take your medicine. But realize this: our life—your life—remains "a mist". Our physical vulnerability remains in spite of our best efforts to protect ourselves. Without diminishing the need to do basic things to protect your physical body, I want to shift your focus to something far more important:

What are you doing to secure the well-being of your soul?

Protecting Our Soul

If you have a long list of habits designed to protect your body from potential harm, do you have, at least, an equally long list of habits designed to protect your soul? I want you to know that security for your soul is available. If I were to summarize Psalm 46, I would say this: *Ultimate security can only be found in God.*

Psalm 46 speaks words of comfort into circumstances that are turned upside down. We are reminded in this Psalm that there are trials that cannot be overcome by specialized skills, material wealth, or clever innovation. In the day of trial, we need something bigger than ourselves. In the day of trial, we need God. This is the grand message of Psalm 46.

Many of you are aware that this psalm inspired Martin Luther's hymn, *A Mighty Fortress is Our God,* and so as we wade through Psalm 46, I want to reference this great hymn.

The first question we need to address, even before we examine this psalm, is whether this is our God. This is an important distinction. The vast majority of Bahamians believe in God. But it's important to see that God is not some ambiguous "higher power". The God described in Psalm 46 is *a personal God*. God is twice identified in the psalm as "the God of Jacob" (Ps. 46:7, 11). This is the God of the covenant. Martin Luther's hymn is even more specific as he answers the question:

Dost ask who that may be? Christ Jesus it is He.

The promises of Psalm 46, then, are for those who truly belong to Christ. What then, are the promises of Psalm 46? We are told, in the plainest of language:

"God is our refuge and strength, a very present help in trouble" (Ps. 46:1).

Or, as Martin Luther has put it: "A mighty fortress is our God, a bulwark never failing; our helper He amid the flood of mortal ills prevailing." What is a "bulwark"? A bulwark is another word for "fortress" or "barricade"—it is a place where people can go to be protected from their enemies. If such a great fortress is available to us, why would we seek refuge anywhere else? Let us not think for a minute that we can overcome the challenges of life by our own power and strength. As Charles Spurgeon has said: "If we look to ourselves for courage we shall fail in the hour of trial". As Martin Luther has written in the hymn: "Did we in our own strength confide, our striving would be losing".

We need something bigger than ourselves if it is to be well with our soul. We need to take refuge in that Mighty Fortress. We need to retreat to that Bulwark never failing. It should bring us tremendous comfort to hear that God is "a *very present* help in trouble." We readily confess that, in a manner, God is always present—everywhere and to every person. To His children, however, God is not simply present, He is "very present". Our God is not watching from the sidelines, but He is actively sustaining us. Spurgeon reminds us that God is even more present than our nearest friend because God is working within us by His indwelling Spirit. It is for this reason the psalmist can write, "we will not fear" (Ps. 46:2).

Our fear is restrained and hedged in by our trust in the promise that God is working all things for our good and His glory (Rom. 8:28). This does not mean, of course, that life will be easy. When the Scripture declares that God is our refuge, this is not a promise of exemption from hardship. The psalmist says (God) is our help in the midst of trouble. The psalmist speaks of trouble, he speaks of mountains being carried into the sea, he speaks of roaring waters, and he speaks of nations in uproar (Ps. 46:2-6).

What we don't see is the psalmist promising a life without hardship. What is promised is Divine comfort and spiritual preservation in the midst of the life's most challenging trials. Again, this is why we can say, "Therefore, we will not fear" (Ps. 46:2).

> ~
> *Our fear is restrained and hedged in by our trust*
> *in the promise that God is working all things*
> *for our good and His glory (Rom. 8:28).*
> ~

It's not that mountains being carried into the heart of the sea doesn't scare us. It's not that our failing relationship doesn't scare us. It's not that our serious medical condition doesn't scare us. It's not that our fragile financial standing doesn't scare us. It's that we understand that our ultimate prosperity—our soul's communion with God—is never in jeopardy. The psalmist wants us to consider something much bigger than trembling mountains and raging waters. In verse 10 the Lord Himself speaks, "Be still and know that I am God. I will be exalted among the nations, I will be exalted in the earth!" The text literally reads, "Cease striving and know that I am God." This is not a command to be idle. This is a command to stop building for ourselves fortresses that do not protect in the day of trial. This is a command to let God do His thing and to have His rightful place as Lord of your life. As Jonathan Edwards has said:

> "In that He is God, He is an absolutely and infinitely perfect being; and it is impossible that He should do amiss."

God will not do amiss in your life. Yes, the mountains may tremble, yes, the waters may foam, but your outward circumstances do not need to determine the outcome of your life. Our God is preserving something far more valuable than your outward circumstances. The Lord is preserving your faith in Him; He is preserving your soul. As the hymn declares, "He will hold you fast". Or, as the late R.C. Sproul states:

> "We are secure, not because we hold tightly to Jesus, but (we are secure) because He holds tightly to us."

Our self-constructed cisterns are merely temporary containers holding temporary blessings. Martin Luther understood this as evidenced in the conclusion of his hymn:

> "Let goods and kindred go, this mortal life also, the body they may kill; God's truth abideth still; His kingdom is forever."

Our God is a mighty fortress to which we can run. Have you ever wondered why, for a period of hundreds of years, church buildings were almost always designed as massive structures? Did you know that, in the Presbyterian tradition, our theology drove the manner of our construction? The walls of St. Andrew's Presbyterian Kirk are estimated to be three and a half feet thick. That's a bit excessive, don't you think? Unless the builder's aim was to have this building remind us, and point us to, a greater fortress.

Our security, of course, is not found in a building. Our security is in a God who calls us to gather in this building to experience the prescribed means of grace. God is a bulwark never failing, but we are exhorted to tether to this bulwark in very particular ways. We tether to this bulwark as we engage the Word of God as it is read and preached. We tether to this bulwark as we baptize and celebrate the Lord's Supper. We tether to this bulwark as we pray and praise together. A mighty fortress is our God! A bulwark never failing!

As we increasingly discover just how vulnerable and fragile we are, this becomes an important reality to cling to. Lock your doors, wear your seatbelt, invest your money, and take your medicine. But please understand that your earthly life remains a mist that is quickly fading. Our true and ultimate security is found in God alone. God will not do amiss in your life your life. He will hold you fast.

- Eplilogue -
Pain In The Pulpit

My goal is God Himself. At any cost, dear Lord, by any road.
- John Owen

It was Sunday morning, about 8:40 am, and I had just pulled out of my driveway when my phone rang. As I drove to St. Andrew's Kirk to officiate Sunday worship a family member from Canada called with the news that my sister had just died. My sister had endured a lengthy battle with cancer, but that did little to diminish the shock of hearing the words, "Bonnie passed away this morning."

The Kirk's Associate Pastor, Chrishon Ducker, was extremely gracious and pastorally sensitive as I shared the news with him of what had transpired. Chrishon offered to look after everything, and to even preach the sermon for me. I insisted, however, that I needed to preach. My text was Psalm 46, under the heading, "A Mighty Fortress Is Our God" (The manuscript for this message is the content of the previous chapter). My comment to Chrishon was, "If I can't preach this text *today* then I can never preach it." We were three weeks removed from the devastation of Hurricane Dorian and I discerned that Psalm 46 would be a suitable text to bring comfort to a community that was badly hurting. Little did I realize how badly I would be hurting as I delivered the sermon.

The pain I was feeling in the pulpit was intense, to say

the least, but I also had an overwhelming sense of God's sustaining grace as I preached. There may be many things I am lacking, but not once have I ever felt shortchanged on grace. Every single Sunday, every single sermon, I experience the strengthening Hand of God's grace. The portion of grace is always enough. On Sunday, September 22, 2019, I was more desperate than usual. Thankfully, God's grace was again sufficient (2Cor. 12:9).

While my pain was particularly acute that Sunday in September 2019, pain is not an uncommon companion in the pulpit. I wonder how many preachers I speak for when I say that I bring my pain into the pulpit more Sundays than not. Behind the veil of God's grace is a frail, and somewhat fractured, human being. I suspect the impact my suffering has had on my sermon preparation and delivery is significant. From family illnesses to family deaths to family feuds, from battles with infertility to everyday stresses of marriage and parenting, from ministry failures to ministry letdowns, from deaths within the congregation to dissatisfied members departing to worship elsewhere, the sources of pain and discouragement are myriad.

Every preacher has a history of pain, which informs and influences his ministry and teaching. There are times when I sense the Holy Spirit overriding that pain to accomplish His purposes, but more frequently I sense the Spirit leveraging my pain to make me more useful for Christ and His kingdom.

Many years ago I read, "The Gift Of Pain" by Dr. Paul Brand. The book emerged from Dr. Brand's work with leprosy patients, which convinced him that pain truly is one of God's great gifts to us. I recall finding Dr. Brand's experiences and testimony compelling, but his assertion that pain is a "gift" didn't resonate with my own experiences at the time. That has changed for me now. As the years advance, I am increasingly able to "connect the dots" between my painful experiences and the manner in which God has shaped, and continues to shape, my character. I have come to embrace pain—not as something pleasant, but as something necessary for my pursuit of Christ-likeness. God's track record in human history, and in my life, is a perfect one. God does not waste pain. The cross of Christ is the greatest example of this. If God can advance His glory through the gruesome death of His Son, He can advance His glory through your pain and mine—and He has. Be assured, God will not do amiss with your pain.

Lord cut, Lord carve, Lord wound, Lord do anything that may perfect your image in me, and make me fit for heaven. Amen.

- For Further Study -

The Crook In The Lot
Thomas Boston

Precious Remedies Against Satan's Devices
Thomas Brooks

Walking With God Through Pain And Suffering
Tim Keller

A Grief Observed
C.S. Lewis

Providence
John Piper

The Loveliness Of Christ
Samuel Rutherford

The Invisible Hand
R.C. Sproul

Surprised By Suffering
R.C. Sproul

Suffering
Paul David Tripp

All Things For Good
Thomas Watson

www.ingramcontent.com/pod-product-compliance
Lightning Source LLC
Chambersburg PA
CBHW071213130726

47998CB00002B/736